Winter Bloom

assorted *poems* about love and lesser things

by Matt Pelicano

Oakdale Publishing, Inc.

Copyright © 2022 by Matt Pelicano

All rights reserved. No part of this book may be reproduced or transmitted in any form or by any means, electronic or mechanical, including photocopying, recording, or by an information storage and retrieval system - except by a reviewer who may quote brief passages in a review to be printed in a magazine or newspaper - without permission in writing from the publisher.

Oakdale Publishing, Inc.

Matt Pelicano
www.mattpelicano.com

**Cover Photograph
by Sandra Stanton**

Publisher's Note: This is a work of fiction. Names, characters, places, and incidents are a product of the author's imagination. Locales and public names are sometimes used for atmospheric purposes. Any resemblance to actual people, living or dead, or to businesses, companies, events, institutions, or locales is completely coincidental.

Summary: *Winter Bloom* is the result of a reawakening of things which had lain dormant. The poems contained herein sing of rebirth; they tell a love story in free verse; and they mark the passage of long, bleak winter into the arms of hopeful spring. Every word was inspired by the mutual discovery taking place between two hearts. If there is a frenzied exuberance characterizing this collection of poetry, then it is the excitement of having found - in the most unlikely of places - everything that the poet never dared hope for. From time to time, the reader hears echoes of passion as unabashed as the most naked emotions penned by E.E. Cummings, or desperation as stark as that of Sylvia Plath. But, above all, there is joy bursting from between these pages! The joy of life, the joy of love, the joy of springtime amid the world's wintering.

1. Poetry – American / General

ISBN/SKU: 9780578386027
ISBN Complete: 978-0-578-38602-7
Publication Date: 3/04/2022

Winter Bloom/Matt Pelicano. -- 1st ed.
ISBN 978-0-578-38602-7

*to Sandra
whose smile
became the promise
to build a life upon*

Table of Contents

Preface 11
Introduction 13
why does it feel like a hundred years 15
when evening wears wintering snowfall 16
you are a landscape of infinite detail 18
i have learned all i will ever need 19
there's not enough room 20
we are binary stars, my love 21
beauty follows your footsteps 22
what is it that holds up these walls? 24
let me tell of a love story 26
'tis an everlasting monday 28
Someone lived in an everywhere way 30
when has winter ever been so still 31
she softens my all with her near 32
you are a church 33
May it always be so 34
how does it feel to know 35
today was spring 36
close your eyes, love; rest your mind 38
you are more beautiful than the night 40
does God still hear these prayers 41
black trees, thick with raucous 42

this brain, as wrinkled as it is wise	44
conceive within this fragment of forever	45
solitude	46
from without, where i too often have to do	48
the ragged earth is razor-burned	49
beneath the winter skylight	51
the mountain breathes with lungs	52
i stood in the cold	54
at times, brief though they be	55
and when i have given my last	56
she dances his joy in the starlight	58
it is as if i wandered into a world	59
let's walk the yellow cobblestones of Paris	60
in tandem we journey	62
i miss you most	63
i first saw your face	64
i love the whats and hows	66
within a winter's walk	67
oh, to know the heart of a bird	68
i delude myself	70
i love you for the way	73
in Paris, by the Seine	75
we make moments together	76
i can(not for lack of trying)	77
each lily-white lily striped	79
i don't mind the cold, my love,	80
shhh…	81
what is this secret garden?	82

for which of my (black as night) sins	83
i will meet you	84
you weave wonder from rain clouds	85
and when this body crumbles	86
in those suspended, timeless	87
if i could fit myself	88
this photograph of faded and worn	90
ah, words!	93
i started a list	94
bring me your thoughts	95
what was it you said	97
we are as old as we aren't young	98
my children,	99
we are prodigious excavators, my love	100
what would i not do to ease your mind?	102
while i'm winding down clocks	103
myGod, myLove	104
in much and how many shades of desire	106
slow down, humanity, slow down!	107
i miss you most	108
i still wear your scarf	109
every	110
i touch taut, trembling tones	111
church bells ring in the distance	112
will i ever run out of words	113
as we speak, sleep steals	114
take my words	115
where do you go?	116

oceans bleed moonbeams	117
i dreamed you were perfect	118
you move in me	119
a gaggle of lost souls	120
there is no silence	121
let the nighttime enfold us	122
flesh stiffens, hardens	123
i awakened to find you	124
take this fleeting	125
there is pain in discovery	126
oh, my child	127
the snow slips	128
where do i begin?	129
why does beauty sting the heart, so?	131
you are so close	132
i must no, more often	135
why should i wonder, as i do?	137
i am a pulsing vein	139
lungs flail	141
if i could but rest my lips	143
i am my father's son	144
at the end of my life	146
Susan, you may never know	148
skin blisters and cracks	150
infinite in reach, beyond knowing	152
green gloss of wax unfolds	154
i shall not, beloved, else but strive	156
the trees stagger	157

i picked a path through fallen leaves	159
spring… it visited me	161
you whisper movement	163
let us weave springtime in winter	165
the withered, black pearls	167
she crouches in shadow	169
snow falls up so downy	171
i see ghosts, phantoms	172
people make places	174
this is but a sunset	175
who are these faces?	176
i feel each mile	177
you said it best, my love	179
'we're higher than the clouds,'	180
the cardinal puffs his plumage like a pout	182
you always start my day	184
winter bloom	186
on winter waters	187
wildflowers	188
whom does the moon love	189
let's take the next plane	190
show me (my darling)	191
know me gradually	192
please do not shield me	193
i have known nothing, too long	194
love? do you think	195
look closely	196
how can i sleep?	197

may we always love	198
are you not the rain?	199
you move through me	200
let's plan to make no plans tomorrow	201
wheres	202
you tricked me	203
is love not pure?	204
the nighttime stains my bare feet	205
spare me	207
feel the brevity of life	209
love is too singular for rhyme	211
Mia's wook-wuck	212
please don't	213
this is where my everyness lives	214
under the cover of darkness	216
they forage in frozen fields	218
you absorb me, like the rain	219
this place has suffered enough	220
i've grown old	222
goodbye, goodbye	223
About the Poet	225

Preface

Writing prose is an architectural endeavor. Every word is a brick fired in the kiln of the imagination, hand-placed with painstaking precision, and affixed using the mortar of sheer willpower. The edifice which takes shape at the end of the pen is baptized in the sweat of the author's brow. Writing prose is hard work, so hard that I often wonder why anyone – including myself – would ever freely choose to engage in such an undertaking.

Writing poetry is altogether different. Whereas prose is wrung from the mind, poetry flows from the heart. Every word is chosen, as a painter chooses from his palette, selecting according to the emotion or mood he hopes to evoke. Poetry is born of effusion, from a trance-like channeling of past experiences. Poetry is alarmingly personal and only thinly veiled in its vulnerability.

What the poet writes he often understands only in retrospect. But understand it, he does, even if only intuitively. And he is healed by both the catharsis of the writing process and by the introspection taking place after the words have been committed to paper.

What the reader understands is only ever her own interpretation. This is why students of poetry who are taught to ask *what the poet was thinking when he wrote this* will forever miss the point of poetry on several different fronts.

First, the poet *feels* his way through the writing process far more than he *thinks* his way through. So, the student attempting to ascertain what the poet was thinking will almost certainly draw a blank.

Second, as I have already mentioned, the poet rarely understands what every line is about until after the fact. In that way, in the end the poet becomes the student, trying to decode what he himself has constructed.

Finally, it is far more gratifying for the poet to think that his work is interpreted according to the needs of the reader than according to the poet's own intentions. If he wanted to make his intentions clear, he would have written prose.

The point of poetry is not to discover *what the poet was feeling (let alone thinking) when he wrote this,* but rather to feel something yourself. A good poem evokes empathy. A great poem opens the heart of the reader to a deeper awareness of his or her *own* emotions. If *Winter Bloom* has this effect, then I am content.

Every single poem contained herein was inspired within me by one woman. These poems constitute a diary of awakening, a chronicle of our love story, a daily journal charting the course of mutual discovery.

Some of these were written to whisper from my heart to hers – even across the crowded room of a published and public work such as this. Some were written because the feelings they contain could not be contained inside the heart any longer. Others were written simply to smile at her, brush my hand against hers, and gain her graceful and elegant attention for a moment. After all, the highest purpose of any work of art is to express love, passion, and admiration – all of which I possess in overabundance for you, my love.

Each poem echoes back to me the emotions I was feeling when I wrote it. Each line speaks to her of the shared meanings only we understand. It is my hope that something within this collection will speak to you, the reader, some of the sentiments your own heart needs to hear, as you listen in on the conversation taking place between the poet and his muse.

Verona, NY   *M.R.P.*
February 14, 2022

Introduction

I have had the privilege of knowing Matthew Pelicano for over 30 years, first as his teacher and now as an "old" friend.

A most astounding thing happens to young, impassioned writers—they become more and more experienced, and then? Passionate writers, only if they have the courage to do so. For words carry a power unlike any other force and the will to use them to their potential must be accompanied by strength, love, and responsibility. Yes, the responsibility of dealing with the aftermath of emotions tapped, shredded even, by the written word.

Matt Pelicano does just that—rips us apart with his poignancy. But we need not assume that he leaves us there, alone. His beautiful rendering of love brings us back from despair to safety, back to a hopeful world that contains a deep, strong regard for the preservation of humanity.

Matt's growth as a poet these many years has brought him to this exquisite height. Believe me, we are truly fortunate that Matthew Pelicano's poetry is in our midst, garnering life-lessons of hope and strength during these uncertain times.

Thank you, Matthew!

Susan Manchester
Poet, Visual Artist

POETRY

why does it feel like a hundred years

why does it feel like a hundred years
since last we kissed?
since last time
stood still,
balanced on the edge
of embrace?
fingers laced
and tangled breath,
inhaling
all you set aside;

a hundred years – no,
more;
never; but for the unmistakable:

i am drowned
and lost –

my all
and ever i was –

in the ocean of your presence;
in the mournful of your absence;
in the all
and ever after
we two shall be.

when evening wears wintering snowfall

when evening wears wintering snowfall
held aloft by the tremulous air,
and darkness wraps us
in quilted contentment
of moonlight and music fair
(for, few things so soothe the soul
as *Clair de Lune*,
or your hand in mine),
from afar, time stands breathless,
looking on;

how sweetly the flickering candlelight
caresses the blushing contours
of your cheek
upon which rests the smile
which ensnared my heart;

(if ensnared, indeed, it be;
for never has it felt so truly free);

i store up stolen glances
for the winter spent apart;

the warmth
of your nearest touch;

the sighs
of your closest heart;

the words
even prying midnight
could not discover;

but, soft!
hear the snow recount
the moment when
first we kissed!

for, would it not know?
did it not see?
and held this,
its treasured secret,
for so long?

break silence, gentle friend,
i give thee leave to tell;

for beauty
must enlighten
every soul;

some to hearten;
while others,
to console.

you are a landscape of infinite detail

you are a landscape of infinite detail;
a bright seascape of boundless abyss;
striations of nuance and meaning,
beneath temples of unending bliss;

a shoreline of calm, hidden harbors;
a lighthouse in wild, whirling mists
of hurricane winds that surround me;
too real for this man to resist;

you're a moonscape of soft, sleepy dreaming;
a sunset of quilted and mine;
a sunrise of whispered tomorrows
for which, every drop of me pines;

i will sail the seas of your memory;
let me cross wide deserts of time,
just to build my home inside you,
that i might forever be thine.

i have learned all i will ever need

i have learned all i will ever need to know of life,
by watching the carefree clouds at play;

at their full-fingerless hands of mindful and present,
i have learned...

of change, and the mutability of all things fact;

of constancy, and the unchanging of all things true;

of the dangers of shaping and reshaping
until nothing left remains;

of the essential of wide, unbroken perspective;

of the poisoning worthless of tribal;

of the hopeless of nothing (no, nothing) at all;

of the necessity of determination in the face of
heedless (ruthless) winds;

of the oneness of irreplaceable you
in the eyes of unrepeatable me;

of the unity of all creatures as they form, reform,
and fade away beneath an ancient, indifferent sky.

there's not enough room

there's not enough room;
not enough space
between these walls;

not enough wide
beneath below, among within;

though i lie on my back,
feet flat against,
my hands upon
these (pushing, stretching,
carving out an empty
from the lovely of your
sweetly contoured form)
the center of the
sided-smoothly,
throbbing-curving,
longing-to-be,
all-of-who-i-am;

i simply cannot
fit the all-and-
every-part of you

inside the all-and-
every-little-heart of me.

we are binary stars, my love

we are binary stars, my love;
cross-armed and hands clasped,
we whirl in an orbit of centrifugal
allure; reciprocal regard;
echoing esteem; and a love
to set worlds in motion;

you are the eye at the core
of my slow-turning all;
the quiet, calm heart of my storm;
you flow like a current of ever-widening,
drawing me, like rainwater
from depths unknown;

we are two flames of one love,
burning; soul-wicks of a sole,
fragrant wax; like mythical trees
of biblical, ancient, eternal renown,
this love burns, but is not consumed;
it gives warmth; ever nurturing love;

you are the epicenter of my
beating heart; the source of my
soul's trembling; the tremor
that roused my mind
from its sleep; the depths
from which arise
all that is deep.

beauty follows your footsteps

beauty follows your footsteps;
a fluttering stream of luminous
butterflies against a sky of frowning
grey; like flecks of fire, sparks ignite
imagination, a conflagration of desire;
i burn for you; the touch of your mind;
the innocence of your heart;
the mastery of all that you are;

with hands that sketch the children
of my mind; and feet that glide
like dazzling swans upon a stage
of sighs; emotion becomes you;
for you are music, herself;
do, let me harmonize;

and, in the secrets of our love,
when i read my words to you,
you close your eyes...

...and my heart resolves itself
to wine upon your lips;

i am dashed upon the rocks
of frustration: is this all that i am?
is this all i have to give?
could i not be more of me for you?
the more to love you with;

how you listen with love
to rival God's very own;
and in my awkward hands
i carry offerings of earthen words;
and your chaste hands
consecrate each one;

like water in wine,
you transfigure the lost and fallen,
giving line to shapeless;
and shade to shadow;

until all you touch
becomes divine,
ennobled, set apart,
for you are, yourself,
a work of art.

POETRY

what is it that holds up these walls?

what is it that holds up these walls?
this slumping roof, suspended like hope
above the fertile ground? where
once a foundation stood, square
as truth, now, fissures belie belief;
the future is ever built on dreams;

like molten rubber, windows bend and
twist beneath the weight of a leaden sky;
held solid by the brown-splatter of
generations beyond recall;

cattle exhale steam in clouds
of dank straw and fermented
sweetness; moisture clinging
to whiskered chins, their plodding
hooves churn mud to bountiful virtue;

a great defeat is afoot;
an epic battle, all but lost;
one brushstroke at a painstaking
time, as picking nails peel back,
layer by bloody layer, the unwritten
record of loss, loss, ample, ever loss;
all years measured in units of lean;

ringed by a mote of pikes, reduced
by scythe and ruin, the old barn
heaves like a great birthing sow;
rolling-to, she shifts her weight

beneath an aging sun,
to wallow in the reward
of her work well done.

let me tell of a love story

let me tell of a love story,
of long ago shared;

of moving through circles in orbits,
always widening, never closing;

ever further, so much farther;
of a time-lost, forgotten;

until all that remained
were two faint, distant names
of two people, who once were,
but no longer the same;

and so,
separately,
we lived, and so
we loved, and so
we dreamed,

and we built,
and we lost,
and we mourned

each by brick, and
beat by heart, as
all things passed away;

but then joy followed surrender;
and contentment sprung from resigned;

until, again, we met for the first time;

two faint, distant names;
two people, who once were,
but now,
at last,
no longer the same;

and how we'd changed:
by moving, altered, through sames
inside of mindful;

by orbiting old ideals
within newness of now-certainty;

always glancing,
never touching;
drawing nearer,
ever nearer;

so much wandering,
so much wondering;
of a time-found,
so unearned;

until all that remained
was to gradually discover

what it means
to call you
by name.

'tis an everlasting monday

'tis an everlasting monday
in which we dwell;
a bleakness of unchanging;
an unbroken succession of wistful;

with words strewn
like stepping stones
across chasms
of dire aspiration;

when your lightest sigh
would surely shatter
the facade endeavoring to replace
the eloquent fluency of touch;

but what can be done,
when mired,
as we are,
in unyielding love?

the more we struggle
to enmesh our hearts,
the deeper we are swallowed
by the greedy gulps
of ever-yearning;

until at last,
like throbbing clots
of bruised and violet,
our hearts claw their way

from nearness to nearness
through a wasteland
of raw separation;

drawing closed
the curtains of the past
behind us;

opening wide
the windward windows
to approaching horizons;

is it a wonder, then,
that, held captive by spiteful suffering -

our eyes opened at last
to the harsh contrast
between then & now,
resignation & hope,
contentment & joy -

we should feel the more,
the more we feel?

that sensitivity should run apace with affection?

that love should place insistent demands
upon the future (all payable presently)?

or that we, in fact,
our own suffering increase,
until we grant this love
the shared life that it seeks?

Someone lived in an everywhere way

Someone lived in an everywhere way;
as more he went, the less he stayed;
and little by little, by much, by small,
Someone began to go nowhere at all;

somehow, somewhere, he'd misplaced his why;
as who and when went where-ing by;
and wonder by ponder, at last, by how,
Someone decided to stop off at now;

he let go of then, he took hold of yet,
tried to recall, never forget;
he opened to maybe, to might, to true;
as olding became renewing his youth;

now Someone lives in a where-he-is way,
as more he discovers, the more he stays;
by loving, and giving, in all, to try,
Someone has (grateful) discovered his Why.

when has winter ever been so still

when has winter ever been so still,
and snowfall so silent?
like the mittened hands
of a clock unwinding, time well spent
is never wasted, but passes (nonetheless)
through our lives and out into memory;

when has the evening shone so blue,
and the sky so starless?
as when snow clouds tussle
treetops, bending (bow-sore) beneath
their frosty loads?
every soul that lives has its burdens,
theirs, no less than ours;

when has the moon ever been so cold,
and bled so white upon the broken landscape?
as when lovers part, and all seems lost,
dramatic - as only a moon can be -
but, still, I hear the nightbird's cry,
for I am this broken landscape, sighing;
far distant across the sky is she.

POETRY

she softens my all with her near

she softens my all with her near;
reclining through mists of awakening,
i'm startled to find this nowness embracing me,
it had always ever been a never was;

and drawing my evening from morning,
as vestal motion, she spins meaning from music,
revealing that which, shy and modest,
had longed to remain unseen;

and what is this wound, this knife-point,
this stabbing, bruised-selfless concern?
why must she wound me with kindness?
why must she slay me with love?

writhe, fortunate heart;
too long have you felt
only the cold-stone of death;
too long have you slept amid specters;
arise now, and cast off your fear;
for her touch is a balm,
and her love ever-near.

you are a church

you are a church of stained glass and sacred;
living flames that dance atop columns of wax,
tethered by sooty wicks to life's ambient seasons;
your presence enraptures my soul at prayer;

kneeling among the heaving rafters,
clouds of incense, like wisps of spirit and shade,
slowly scatter a million drops of acrid pain;
healing, calming, freeing; and I do not mind
if sometimes evening becomes longing;

with you, all is hushed, suspended, at peace;
for, to speak would be to transgress a hallowed silence,
to break the commandment to love;
and to Whom should I turn?
yours are the words of life ever-after;
yours, the wounds by which I am made whole.

in the dark, by the light of a solitary flame;
awash in grace and worship,
I dare to whisper your name;
for, I do not mind
if sometimes living feels like dreaming.

May it always be so

May it always be so,
or, if not May,
then springtime,
when morning
dawns crocus,
and winter
turns to thaw;

or, if not May,
and if not morning,
then wintertime, only;
and, oh my love, do let it be
the eighteenth day of December,
let it be so, a month at a time;

and, as we watch the falling snow
descend to earth upon frosted wing,
i'll warm your heart in wintertime,
and it shall always be our spring.

how does it feel to know

how does it feel to know
that you are the answer to a prayer?
an answer spoken through silver,
whispered through moonlight,
descended like dew through the air?

how does it feel to know
that God had a solution in mind
for all my yearnings,
my insistent pleadings,
my vast, consuming
(it could only be) empty,
and the solution held,
cradled in His mind, was you?

then, leaning forward,
through a cloud of indignant,
through a swarm of impertinent,
He touched my lips, saying,

"Hush, child. Be at peace.
The moment was waiting for you.
For I AM, and She is, now you must be, too."

today was spring

today was spring

(i don't think winter objected,
needing a day off for errands and such,
Christmas is always too near)

is it not strange to hear
so many singing birds
and see none at all?

what season will tomorrow bring, musing?

(i hope for another like today's,
for it is then that
"young man's fancy
lightly turns to thoughts of love"
or some such Tennyson)

but i would settle gladly
for one sliver of May;

a pleasant thought, that,
if May does not object to being parsed
for my pleasure;

but you, being two weeks my senior,
have seen more winter than i,
and yet, it has not chilled your sweetly heart;
remarkable soul, irrepressible spirit,
warmth of a million sunsets.

i have no illusion that winter
will not return; i feel its ever-approach,

the dry cracks forming between us;
the arresting grip
of goodbye in my lungs;

but for now, let me live in spring
where forever blooms
and the first blush of robins sing.

close your eyes, love; rest your mind

close your eyes, love; rest your mind;
there is safety in this ragged world,
this place of wrest and squander,
this field of howling waste;
for you, it is here with me,
safe within my arms,
asleep so near my heart;

i will not drift, i will not slumber
through this, my sacred watch;
do not trouble yourself
with worries, no,
not even on my account,
though kind be your
loving concern;

it is not sleep i desire,
but a chance to love,
a moment for which
to live ennobled;
and by loving, to flood
your heart and mind
with certainty so sweet,
as to make wildflowers grow;

let your dreams wander,
give them free reign
to break upon green pastures
of light, full galloping sunshine,
wild, windy, breathless flight;

whatever the fleet sun touches,
however wide the endless
horizon spreads,
all is yours,
all was made
to be thine,
all things
with your name,
to rhyme;

these are not
words to woo;
they are not
snares of seduction;
these are words of reborn,
truths to build a life upon,
sprung from soil tilled by
blunt, throbbing pain;
watered in the blood of suffering,
and now grown to full season
by the touch of your tiny hands;

so, while you sleep; while your mind is lithe,
and your heart attentive to the sound of my voice,
hear me whisper my confession in the night;
hear me speak of moments,
strung like strings of pearls,
one by next by other,
minutes by hours to days become lifetimes;
there is no other stuff of which lives are made;

but, oh how we might fashion them!
oh, how we might love!
for life is the shortest of all passing seasons,
and love is the noblest and worthiest of reasons.

POETRY

you are more beautiful than the night

you are more beautiful than the night,
tragic though she is, lying guiltless
at the feet of sunset and westering;
day's death is but a passing thing,
your beauty is eternal;

you are more lovely than the dawn,
who stands astride his vanquished foe;
a prideful youth, no more aware
of the shortness of time than
of the grandeur of kindness;
but, you shine forth compassion,
as the moon reflects the sun;

you are more delicate than the sea's fragile foam
born of the tumult of sand and surf;
how strange, that fury begets fragility;
for, in your strength, lay hidden,
more delicate things than
my bruised heart dare behold;

you are more perfect than all brokenness,
which bears the image of our lives,
the wounds through which our
selfishness was surrendered;
once shattered,
we are refashioned, again,
into the highest heights of perfection
one might ever hope to achieve:
that of imperfect you for imperfect me.

POETRY

does God still hear these prayers

does God still hear these prayers
of clapboard and weatherworn?
of tar-paper bare? of mislaid moss
and mold-eaten tile? could even
He see through this flowing glass;
thicker nearest the ground;
paper-thin up where angels abound;

the handrails, guiding worshippers
carefully up unshakeable steps,
tickle irony to laughter; for, once inside,
beneath the splintering rafters,
enclosed by crumbling walls,
these same cautious Christians
are much nearer, my God, to thee
than their faith gives eyes to see;

and whence this stolen steeple?
this cross-crowned belfry?
God's lightning rod?
was it pawned for ransom,
long ago? or melted for musket
shot, to save a nation's soul?
at what cost, this union;
this spire? these young lives lost?
the innocents of an age
sprung like poppies from the virgin snow.

black trees, thick with raucous

black trees, thick with raucous;
dripping leaf, seed, stem, and foul;
below the bending, bobbing branches,
i cringe with terror, head down and
sheltering from the stormcrow;

the evening breeze,
like mother's hand, unseen,
cups boughs in bouncing
baby lullabies; or like

a wild, white-haired,
rouge-faced conductress
taming unchained melodies
for the masses from
the throats of a murder
of orchestral crows;

sprinkled like saltpeter
in a peppery wound,
red-winged blackbirds wear
twin stripes like corporals proud;
bright gashes against a necrotic
smudge of crow; rags of black gauze
flutter like heartbeats in the wind;

the evening snow, a contrast in drab;
a study in Poe, the tree creaks ominous,
"nevermore, nevermore;" while i,
with camera eye, seek to steal

the blackbird's soul; when off fly
bashful ravens, loathe to
lend me their likeness awhile;

but, up in the shuddering tree,
released at last from cramped
and swarming throng,
the red-winged blackbirds pause;

in silent surrender, born aloft
on the unaltered air, they yield
their winter souls to me;
a contrast in graceful poise;
a study in peaceful ecstasy.

this brain, as wrinkled as it is wise

this brain, as wrinkled as it is wise;
smooth as a chicken breast, boneless
and quivering; a gelatin of confusion;
a ponderous pudding of slow pondering;
it stiffens in my skull; perhaps,
it has lived there too long;

beneath this roof, this gilded dome -
thinning, thinning, nearly gone...
taking with it all the clumps
that tendrilled roots could grasp -
this waning garden grows to seed;
enriched by the dawdling decay
of thought; things i never sowed bloom
strange among the stepping stones;

wheel ruts, worn by donkey carts
of foolish, scarred the thoughts
of my youth; now backfilled, leveled,
and healed by the calloused hands
of woe; few things etch the brain
so grave as tender mortality;
too few ever learn this truth;
too few ever learn;

between these all-too-narrow ears,
strewn among the cats and clutter;
the passports and photos;
these self-amused snippets
of poems and half-written books;
a new wisdom now wrinkles my brain;
that love and wisdom are truly one and the same.

conceive within this fragment of forever

conceive within this fragment of forever,
this treacherous, jagged shard of now
how many tomorrows today might bring,
how much unknown lay hidden behind unseen:
but what do we really see,
beyond the dreams our eyes conceive?

the could haves of infinite crossroads,
the should haves, like calloused indictments,
the would haves of feeble excuse -
which, taken together, comprise
an un-life, a near-life, a might have been
if-only-life of thin, wispy aspect,
nothing more and never again;

framed within a single orbit,
we strain to add meaning to menial,
purpose to commonplace,
and love to Before -
After, often proving too late.

in echoing soundless,
if courage casts wide
the net of heart-open,
(wherein, we see)
a tiny, frail sunrise blooms
against the infinite horizon,
revealing all these tomorrows
were really, only ever today.

solitude

solitude;
cold as drifted desolation
on a lake where anguish
goes to die; the wind wails
hostile, with frozen flagrance,
she probes the secret spaces
where, once, my body clung to life;

i liquify; eyes tear at the touch
of harsh winter's dry breath; she
handles all things tender too roughly;
even my nose runs to outstrip her;
when only spring could hope to win;

a torso stands, limbless, leafless,
lifeless in the wrinkled fist
of brutal waters, once-liquid, now
stone; strangling the stifled
struggle; stripped bare
beneath translucent ice;
plundered modesty, the final affront;

ringing the shore like heartless
spectators, shrubs bristle wild
with morbid curiosity, straining
their broken necks to glimpse
the captive corpse;

my gorge rises at the sight
of so much grim despondent;

so much bleak and barren;
for, even the mountains
surrender to the scene;
while, beneath the biting snow,
one, hopeful crocus
strives to break free.

POETRY

from without, where i too often have to do

from without, where i too often have to do,
i call to you, call to you; echoing through
a muddle of pining calendars; echoing through
a chaos of longing eagerly; and i wonder,
do you always, darling, hear my voice?

from within, where i too often have not been,
i speak to you, speak to you; running low
on adjectives, images; running out of
reasoning arguments; and i wonder,
my love, do i even have a choice?

from alone, where i too often have to roam,
i think of you, think of you; everywhere i'm
finding you, seeing you; everyday i'm
missing you, needing you;
and i wonder, now,
what was i like
before i loved you?

the ragged earth is razor-burned

the ragged earth is razor-burned;
stiff stubble chafes the cheek of the wind,
caressing, as she does, her lover's face;
the sun sets soonest, these days; 5 o'clock
shadows are lengthening;

among summer's severed stalks,
blackhead crows, like moles
marring unblemished faces, burden
the morning air with their rowdy,
strident screeches; would that the sky
might, pillowing, smother them whole;

in laundry heaps of soiled and dismal,
winter's raiment huddles fast
against the warmth of a fuller
who seeks to bleach them bare;

who knows what treasures lurk
within the folds and pockets
of core-frozen snowbanks: shopping
carts and sundry lives swept up
by indiscriminate snowplows;
a heart, once thawed, reveals all things;

the field, too, is a graveyard of markers;
rows and aisles of unforced perspective;
husks of withered skin; ears of gnawed
and toothless; unfit to swallow by any
but the gluttonous mud; i lose my eye

inside a maze of amazement;
who plants with such precision?
who masters the indifferent ground?

is this not a metaphor?
is it not like a simile?
that i might walk so far afield
to master the seasons
within me.

beneath the winter skylight

beneath the winter skylight,
stars appear
in velvet pinpricks of curiosity;

where could we hope to hide
from an enveloping sky?

a whisper in my ear,
"Look at the stars with me,"

and, around us two,
pushing-up against our feet,
all the earth spins (slowly)
tomorrow into goodbye
beneath the winter skylight,
beneath a weeping sky.

the mountain breathes with lungs

the mountain breathes with lungs
of foothill and floodplain;
upon its slopes, fir trees spread
wide their feathered fingers,
gathering hope sopping
white with purity;

a river of relentless mist flows,
three feet atop the matted floor;
weaving, wafting, weeping its
sluggish way around all in its
path; fox and hare drown
in gossamer veils - hung
lifeless above the gurgling ground;

grey run the watercolor hues,
down dense windowpanes
of sky and unbroken; vistas
spread like bridal trains,
less costly but more assured;

the sullen landscape wears upheaval,
a mad portrait of disproportionate;
rendered in Neo-Topsyturvism,
the sky surges like turbid seawater,
while earthen tides
reclaim the fallen leaves;

along mystic pathways, geese cry
desperate in the creeping fog;

their feet ache to feel the sponge
of safe landing; never were souls
less suited for flight than water
fowl above this fluid plain;

oh, how i fear the sun has died;
how pale he looks in yonder sky.

i stood in the cold

i stood in the cold
outside your heart,
while you lay sleeping inside;

wanting so much to awaken you,
if only to say goodbye;

to kiss your forehead,
to feel your warmth,
to linger a while in your dreams;

i stood in the cold
outside your heart,
where my own heart
longs to be.

at times, brief though they be

at times, brief though they be,
i slip from off my meaning,
i lose the why of me;

perhaps i spend too long & lonesome
dredging through my soul;

perhaps i'm mired in whats & hows
or trying to be whole;

perhaps i muse 'perhaps' too much,
perhaps i always will,

and never hope to satisfy
the whys i try to fill.

and when i have given my last

and when i have given my last,
i immerse myself in nothing,
there, to find, anything
that nothing might give;

and when all these words fail
to return joy to my heart,
echoing vacant in these pillaged ears,
i seek inspiration
in the cold, wet hollows
of the earth;

as low pressure
invites the storm clouds,
obscuring the sun in its sky,
i cannot hope to see myself
except seen through nature's eyes;

nor clear these clouds, distorting,
but on a windy day;
for i am the sun,
of many, just one,
and the many have much to say;

as the fell hunter's presence
is always known
long before he sets eyes
on his prey,
i must stalk and find
that which haunts my mind,

that which knows what my heart
must say;

ah, but where does the lonely
and lovely lake go,
when she has given her all,
and, herself, has run low?

she dances his joy in the starlight

she dances his joy in the starlight,
tracing the paths of fairies and sprites
on a dark, sylvan stage of snowfall,
she moves through the sacred night;

he scribbles pale roses of longing
to scatter beneath her graceful feet;
from his place in the wings, he is hopeful
that, in time, their hands might meet;

around them, the rhythms of living,
play out as simply as elegant song;
between them,
he has become morning,
while she, a poem of dawn.

it is as if i wandered into a world

it is as if i wandered into a world
where everything within me
has been ordered,
        sorted,
        placed with loving care
upon the shelves and mantlepiece of my heart;
        a place for everything,
        now everything in its place;
and your gentlest hands have arranged me;

it is as if i lost myself within
the fragrant forest of days,
when i only ever knew the tenuous now
of so many shattered thens;
        the shadows conceal tomorrow -
        i see it, i swear that it's true -
        it steps aside, but for a moment;
        we wait a while for you;

it is as if i'd been entrusted to your care
by some unknown -
        who am i to say?
        how am i to know?
        i should be ashamed to ask -
until the time was as it should be,
        and you,
        and i, too;
imagine my surprise to be found here,
all along, with unexpected you.

let's walk the yellow cobblestones of Paris

let's walk the yellow cobblestones of Paris,
hand-in-hand and lovers by Seine,
descending below the street-level noise
of nothing - which man pursues;
we'll pick up the discarded pieces of
wilted flowers, cast aside by love's lovers lost,
and plait them into circlets to crown these smiles,
relying only on your hand in mine,
and the sweet, mindful river's flow;

from her wrought iron balcony, la jolie parisienne
writes her sonnets on sycamore leaves,
releasing them - floating down, down, upward, down;
scooping the air like a pendulum on the breeze -
until the broad parchments pour
bitter emotions into the beleaguered Seine;
how many words in how many tongues
must such a literal stream as this endure?

shuffling, heal to toe, to old, to forgotten,
an elderly couple sits down to feed the birds;
their fingers, gnarled like anguished tree limbs,
intertwine as naturally as their years;
oh, what their darkening eyes have contained,
their tired minds have since misplaced;
soon, all that will remain of them is love;

shall we rest our waning youth a while
and count the tangled, jumbled lovers' locks
weighing the weary bridges down,

as the world spins history around us?

there is the obelisk of Egypt,
its fractured base heaving beneath
the corpulence of ages past;
there is the endless parade of arches
vaulting o'er the chalky stream;
there, the eyesore tower, made iconic by time;
here, the storybook lovers, weaving Us out of rhyme;

but where the tyrants of old?
where the warmongers,
moldering with the blood of children?
where the conquerors, victorious but a moment?
they've all gone the way of vile, gaping hate,
and gasp muddy lungs-full of ignorance,
the least of all - which man pursues;

look! see the moonlight dance
across the alabaster skyline;
watch the strobe lights –
diamond fire - race upon the tower;
above aging lovers, Paris sighs,
and blushes rose across the sky,
but it has never read a story
such as ours.

in tandem we journey

in tandem we journey,
if by mile and
where by see,
the last up ahead,
the next left behind,
beyond which,
the more begets the farthest,
but to such shores as this,
few ever arrive;

in the sighing of the trees,
we remember
how wandering
destinations dissolve,
all journeys being treks
of endless discovery;
the closer we draw,
the further we drift,
the deeper we long
to perceive;

but where do i wander
when i'm not by your side?
where, but
towards you, it seems;
for, if delving discovery
be our one true goal,
we pursue it on
circular streams.

i miss you most

i miss you most
in morning,
when missing most
is soon,
and longing steals
like shadows
through the lateness
of my room;

if only missing
morning wore
the harsh
distracted noon,
i'd bravely stride
toward nightfall,
and escape this
morning gloom.

i first saw your face

i first saw your face
so many lifetimes ago,
beyond the horizons
of forgotten youth,
when was - was, not yet so,
and might-be had not yet dreamt
of ever-wondrous this;

                        i first saw your face,
            but did not yet think to know
                          that the you i saw
                        would one day be
            the you whom you now show;

(we knew, we two,
but what we knew
was neither quite yet me,
nor was it quite yet you);

                        i then saw your face
                 (full-blossoming smile)
                  come from the mists
                      beyond all could,
                      beyond all would,
               beyond all reason why,

and sit in quiet hearing,
this heart to comprehend,
and when i saw your sweetest face,
this heart began to mend;

and, in the turning of one evening,
when timid turned from shy,
when caution turned to wonder,
(and wonder wondered why),

i first saw your face
look in love at mine
and all our un-shared yesterdays
at last, made sense to me,

for the face i'd known
from long ago
bore the smile
i'd always need.

POETRY

i love the whats and hows

i love the whats
and hows of you,
the wheres
that you once knew;

and as i learn
the many whys,
i love your reasons, too.

within a winter's walk

within a winter's walk,
i thought of you;

snow-blanketed hills, kissed
blue, beneath the skylight,
made pale by the waning moon;

deep valleys,
still wet with autumn,
through which i stroll
among the evergreens;
the yester-beens;
the ever-new;
and seek to lose myself within
these forests of endless you;

sighs, like the white
wings of snowbirds,
flutter feathers
in my heart,
descending in silence
through the glassy air;

and, though my here
can't reach your there,
within this winter's walk, my love,
i feel you everywhere.

oh, to know the heart of a bird

oh, to know the heart of a bird -

to breathe the effervescent everything
through which i might sail unhindered;

to stretch my wings in freedom most wild,
and surmount the clamoring tumult below;

to choose without compulsion,
and make my home in snowcapped
boxes of man's own devising;

or, unburdened by captive need,
to sing // bare-faced and unashamed \\
among branches of God's fashioning;

to be what i am…

(pause a while,
upon those words)

to be
what
i
am…

to be nothing less
than i am;

and (God help me)

not a needless feather more.

no,
i wish not
more than this;

for foolish wishes
betray want
in him
who'd speak
such a misguided
wish.

i delude myself

i delude myself,
thinking that they know me;
that they mean me no harm;
love me, like i do;
tender feelings of precious
and unblemished;

we have an understanding,
an arrangement;
i fairly take what i want,
and leave them
less than their share;

inside, they feel
my thuds and thumps,
as graceful as a black bear foraging;

in front, between the cramped slit
and the bluebells
near the garden shed,
traffic flurries an organized route
of unseen crossing guards,
yielding to no one;
i know enough to duck,
avoiding the rush hour chaos;
all else, i think i know,
but they know better;

each box upon box sits,
breast-high, upon cement blocks;

and bravely i approach
in veil and gloves;
incense for the offering,
to soothe the goddess
of black and yellow striped;
would that they were less clever
(men, perhaps) and more easily
lulled to sleep;

as i puff grey and acrid,
a hum rises within, pitching up
in ancient words
of warning, as if to say,

"Hmmm, we know you of old;
we know what you're about;"

workers waggle and wriggle down deep,
surrounding that which
every race values most:
survival, a hope for the future,
mother and child;

i wrench the lid rudely,
shattering propolis
like splattering antiseptic amid
the madness of an emergency room,
i heed none of the warning signs;

before my eyes, she appears;
beauty ever old, ever new;
tireless ambition,
selfless dedication
to a cause
fifty thousand strong

and growing by the minute;

i see her;
no veil to clothe her modesty,
for she has breached my defenses,
as only sweetness can,
through a hole near my heart,
and speaks to me,
face to face,
eye to eye,
nose to dagger,
until her point
i receive;
and abandon
my scheme
to thieve.

POETRY

i love you for the way

i love you
for the way your lips curve
into delicate rays of moonbeam;
for the way your hair becomes
soft, velvet night
and tangles itself
in the bare beauty
of a kiss;

i love you
for the way your eyes
invite me to the precipice
of heart and forever;
the way heaven
blushes in your presence
and revels in the part it played
in such a love as this;

i love you
for the way your fingertips
become me,
without separation enough
for the slightest
sigh of spirit;
the way your elegant
(tiniest) finger arches,
descends, and marks the moment
of love's realization
that all is grace,
you no less than the angels.

i love you
for the way your eyes
see the world
and everything it contains
(most generously, me);

for the way your heart
perceives beauty
in the movement
of a blade of grass
bent beneath
a solitary snowflake;

for the way you strive
always to be faithful
to the stirrings
of your heart;

for the way you
let me love
(always) you;
(everywhere) you;
(in every way) you;
(for all my days) you.

in Paris, by the Seine

in Paris, by the Seine,
between le Pont Neuf
et le Pont des Arts;
on la Rive Droite,
le Quai du Louvre;

there is a small rise
of the cobblestone
promenade, beneath
iron rings once used
to moor the boats & barges
(which still heave upon
chalk-brown waters);

atop this rise,
a park bench waits;
upon which, I would,
everyday, sit
and speak to my journal
such secrets as the Seine
will never forget;

i will take you there
that she might meet
the sweetest secret
my heart now keeps.

we make moments together

we make moments together,
(so you and so me)

we turn minutes to hours,
while the hours turn we,

our moments are few
but this won't always be,

for i love much more you
than i'll ever choose me.

i can(not for lack of trying)

i can(not for lack of trying)
get close enough to touch
the furthest fringes
of your nearest heart;

                                  (almost, being a cruel
                                distance most infinite)

do you withdraw from me,
adding inches to miles,
and miles to never?

or does the jaunty earth pirouette
beneath your dancer's feet,
rending us apart,

                                  quite centrifugally
                                  (a word better
                                  suited to prose),
                                  or subtractively
                                  (a word, not at all)

always, one
and one
from two?

how else might i approach you,
other than as i have done?
as friends? as companions?
as strangers? (we have never been)

but, would you not concur,
(in gentle fairness)

that our approaches proceed
from all and every direction, concurrent?

as the present approaches the future;
or daytime, the night?
we move toward one another
like a single foregone conclusion;

whence this frustration, then?
whence this final inch
                              (with tiny limbs of
                              unseen and everywhere)
that holds us,
arm's length, apart?

unless, by distance,
i should come to see
the ever-nearness
of your heart.

each lily-white lily striped

each lily-white
lily, striped
peppermint crimson,
opens, one by one,
by next, by all;

arise morning glorious!
each delicate,
fragrant poem
whispers spring and
remembrance,
for only sleep forgets;

love
and the
awakening of lilies
are forever.

i don't mind the cold, my love,

i don't mind the cold, my love,
if sometimes colder means closer,
when closer always means us;
a warmer fire, there could never be;

these hands of mine are just like
those i used to own, but long ago
when they were warm and young,
paled by the cold northern sun

(a misnomer, to be sure;
see how the snowflakes fall unaltered
through sluggish, blue sunbeams?)

i don't mind the cold, my love,
and, no, i don't think
that our lips would freeze,
but do, let's chance it,
all the same.

shhh...

shhh...

look closely;
uncover each petal;

draw near and listen
with ancient heart
and newborn dreams;

these are not mere
tokens of affection,
but the sacraments
of a sacred promise;

the perennial seeds
of evermore;

and upon each
slender leaf
are written
the chapters
of our
love.

what is this secret garden?

what is this secret garden?
this high-walled courtyard enclosed?
these stones in sudden disarray?
where brambles grow wild in their midst?

what is this place of calm and innermost,
long since bequeathed to neglect?

who carved these hidden pathways?
these well-worn patterns, engraved?
who was it shaped these hedgerows,
where, once, young lovers kissed?

why labor so, if not to cherish?
why admit such sadness, unchecked?

come, let us set things aright;
come, let's rebuild what was marred;
for the world is grown thick with anguish,
from deep inside each wounded heart.

POETRY

for which of my (black as night) sins

for which of my (black as night) sins
are you proof of my redemption?

for which of my seasons of selfishness
are you radiant spring?

for, make no mistake, love,
it pains me to say it,
but you're not what
such wicked things bring;

but, if (sometimes) the eyes
of your generous love
see that which your heart does perceive,
remember this, my dear,
and honesty's preserved:

that, all virtue,
the beloved
from his lover
receives.

i will meet you

i will meet you
on this limb
of our undoing;

i will meet you more
than you might
want me to
at all;

and, if the limb
should start to crack,

i wouldn't dream
of turning back,

but rather,
tumbling first,

i'll surely
break
your
sudden
fall.

you weave wonder from rain clouds

you weave wonder from rain clouds,
and magic from movement,
with fingers of slender refrain;

through a black & white photo,
you contrast all meaning
against that which your heart
might contain;

in your eyes, i am learning
to see subtle sunsets
which melt down
a canvas of sky;

in your heart, i am longing
to see dawn awaken
a love that you
cannot deny.

and when this body crumbles

and when this body crumbles,
as my mind so often does,

and the last word springs fruitless
from this heart,

do not lay me down
in hallowed ground,

for hallowed have i rarely been;

nor in some stone enclosure,

the world being littered
with dull sentiment;

and engrave not upon my grave, not
my bruised and bloodied name, not
these bookend, tidy dates, so unmeaning;

but move at once to forget me,

for forgotten, in time, i will soon be;

for, if my love for you
was not memorable,
then, in faith, love,
remember not me.

in those suspended, timeless

in those suspended, timeless
minutes of barely infinite;

when not quite meets at last,
and the ethereal flame flickers
beneath the slightest sigh of breath;

in those mystical grains of moonlight,
scattered across celestial seas,
against our all too sudden amazement;

i feel as if nothing at all,

or everything at once
could surely be,

and care little
for anything

beyond this
our momentary
kiss.

if i could fit myself

if i could fit myself
inside the delicate
room of your heart -

mahogany walls of
fragrant and warm;

where heart and hearth
are one, and rain
taps rhyme & rhythm
against fragile windowpanes;

i'd curl up, catlike,
in the shadows
of corner-walls and
forgotten; a while
to sleep, a while
to dream, a while
to simply be
among the phantoms
in your heart;

perhaps you'd
sleep best
if i were there
to whisper
calm soothing
in the hollow starless;

and in the night,

when i awoke
to find you
clothed in firelight,

i'd sit in rapt
silence, a while
to pray, a while
to weep, a while
to wonder why

i could not
stay there
for all time.

this photograph of faded and worn

this photograph of faded and worn,
this image of lifeless held captive;
too much sunlight and time lapsed
have rendered it distant;

like a rowboat let out to sea
by a single, frail length of rope,
i have drifted beyond reach
of this moment, whose meaning
is lost in the mists of memory;
i languish at the tiller;
do pull me in;

still, each day i sit and gaze;
each day, i feel its echo aching
through the halls of dire questioning;
what was it i once possessed?
the same did i lose;
what sort of man was this?
the same did i lose;

and around my heart, a crown of thorns;
around my soul, incredulity demands
an accounting, a reckoning of its (God
help me) Creator; why? as if knowing
would make death rational; or life
bearable; or eternity desirable
apart from you; it would not,
i say; it would not; such lies
are terrors for children;

why endow reason,
if only to suspend its use?

why enable me to wonder,
if only to bequeath an excuse?

why equip the soul with wings,
if only to clip and watch it fall?

why ennoble the heart with love,
then permit no love at all?

it's not enough to affirm such things
are beyond the mind of man;

if i carry the divine spark in my heart,
then i was present before i began;

and i stare back at me in silence;
a young man ebbing; i wane
through cycle by cycle of midnight
and weathering; i close
like the fingers of a flower,
gripping life as it slips from my grasp;

i age beyond doubt - if only that were true;
for doubt and fear cannot be outrun,
i've lived long enough to be certain
of this and only this;
of only this, and love;

leaning in, i listen long;
the lips, as yet, i know;
the voice, imagined,

is still my own;
the wisdom,
at best, on loan;

i bid me, "please, do speak to me;"

an answer, i give at last:
"you must, one day,
tear-up this image
as time has torn the past."

ah, words!

ah, words!

so agile and unbounded,
painting murals in the mind,

evoking life and love
and death and forever
from scribbled marks upon a page;

to wield you like a blazing brand
and smite the hide of passing things
is a timelessness beyond the pale!

ah, words!

ah, me!
what a frail and feeble friend,
you've proven to be;

for, against all the words
at my command,
i fail, alas,
to describe thee.

i started a list

                                        i started a list
                                of the things
                      we should do;

                 in no time,
          it grew, and
      it grew, and
it grew, until,

taking a look,
      i discovered
           the truth,
                that no list
                      could replace

                            all of life
                                lived with
                                      you.

POETRY

bring me your thoughts

bring me your thoughts,
of twilight and morn;
i want to bathe in the clear
waters of your mind,
beneath a white,
winter's star;

or, if your thoughts be muddied,
let the coarse sediment
of confusion polish
this jagged heart,
that it might gleam
with the soft brilliance of you;

oh, that i might wander o'er
the well-worn paths
of ponder and aware,
picking wildflowers
from the roadside;

and, with a buttercup
held to my chin,
may i, before the end,
find the answer
to love's great question;

dear heart,
in season and out,
let me always
listen with the mind of a friend,

keep faith with the lips of a confidant,
and never endeavor to repair;

for, broken as i am,
the best i can tender
is my presence,
such as it is;

but, oh, let me love you
with the heart of a soulmate;
and call nothing but this
by the name of love.

what was it you said

what was it you said,
when (whispering) you breathed
love and undying
through the far reaches of my heart?

what was it i heard?
for i rarely trust myself
to understand aright;
you are so much more than i,
so much here, so much life;

how came you by these,
your compelling, astounding words?

i know: you listened,
for you listen
like none other
i have only ever heard;

you listened and,
what it was you learned,
you spoke - in time - to me;

and now look what you've done;
i lay blame, yes, it's true;
(but, would i'd been as brave
as a hundred thousand yous)!

we are as old as we aren't young

we are as old as we aren't young,
even more so, i believe; as for me,
i grow youngest by the sweetness
of each breath i take, stolen,
as they often are,
from you (wouldn't mind,
i thought it true);

we are as living as we love, i think,
for love means living with our everything,
and holding back our nothing from the ones
who give our living love in turn;

just maybe, loving most means
living much by more;

and then, there's you...

as sweet as you are gentleness,
     as kind as you are loveliness,
          more resonant than thoughtfulness,
    possessing love and life and youthful
most by more;

just maybe,
you mean most
the grace of
love's allure.

my children,

my children,

the goal will always be
farther than it appears;

the effort required, greater;

the fear of the thing, worse by far;

and the rewards, beyond all expectations!

we are prodigious excavators, my love

we are prodigious excavators, my love;
archaeologists and delvers of the deep;
moles, if you will permit the comparison;
although, perhaps, it dulls the edge of romance;
though, i care not much, for words
increasingly fall inexcusably short of you;

we dig among the foundations and basements
of our hearts; not to plunder their treasures;
not to squander their wealth; and never, no
never to lay bare their long-buried bones;

we hollow out the old, sifting with care
through the trove of trinkets, the rich
and commonplace, collections of musty,
dust cloths and baubles; more precious
than decades of life lived
long, then all but forgotten;

until, at once and unforeseen,
the well-worn floor falls away,
revealing unknown endless
and unfathomable, whose echoes
we'd never sounded in the deep;

whose paths we'd never trodden;
whose walls we'd never known
had held aloft the floors and ceilings,
beams and windows of our hearts;

but, fear not the fall,
my love, fear not;
for, by casting off this solid floor
we open depths of hidden love
we two might now explore.

what would i not do to ease your mind?

what would i not do to ease your mind?
to lift the sagging load from your back,
bent as it is beneath the weight of worry?

you have toiled alone for so long,
beating back the pace of perversity,
the world's cunning whispers
wrapped in smiles of familiar treachery;
no one wounds like loves past;
such scars never heal;

what would i deny you?
though, it's true, you never asked this of me;
you wouldn't, would you?
how could you, and still remain you?

no, you'd take this burden upon yourself,
as you always have; as i never want you to again;
such things are for the young;
and we are only young at love;
our bodies belie the truth;
some of life has passed beyond our strength;

what else could i do, beloved?
the responsibility is mine;
for, does love not long for commitment?
does commitment shrink from a test?
if i would be worthy to call you my own,
then love must not be merely spoken,
it must be valiantly shown.

while i'm winding down clocks

while i'm winding down clocks
'til midnight, would I want
(wholeheartedly) to hear your voice?
would i? without the slightest doubt
of misunderstanding,
i would, i say,
surely, i would!

and then, just like
(what, i don't know,
for words escape me
in the darkest wonders
of the wee hours of the year)
we are, at one, together;

and i pause just to hear
your breathing;
your heartbeat;
your thoughts, now spoken;
and the night is all
silence and timeless,
suspended as we are
between two years;
the old and the new;
such past and approaching;
'til i fall asleep
cuddling a smiling
pillow.

myGod, myLove

myGod, myLove,
your beauty is pain;

it slays me,
it pierces,

it flays me
alive; or is this
how it feels
when a man
slowly dies?

have mercy,
dear heart,
have
mercy,
i cry!

even
        death
                can
                    not
                        spare
                                me
                        from
                  coming
          alive,

when
i'm

watch
-ing
you

d
      a
            n
      c
e

,

&

i
,

m

d
y
i
n
g

      in
           si
      de
...

POETRY

in much and how many shades of desire

in much and how many shades of desire
does this, my only ever heart for you, roam?

in the mild cycle of your seasons, i journey
a year's breadth - around again -
between spring's fragile morning
and winter's drowsy night;

while, the too feverish heat of summer,
you reserve for more practical things;

(as for me, autumn will always hold sway;
in particular, a bare three days nigh,
before the solstice twilight set;
therein, let me live out my unbroken days);

what is it that i desire the most?
what shape and shade comprise
the landscape of this, my heart of hearts?

it is far less than seasons;
far fewer than months;
for such things cannot
be measured out in lives;

rather, it is the simple, calm desire
of sitting with you by the fire,
while, outside, winter snowflakes
sprinkle the flowers of spring.

POETRY

slow down, humanity, slow down!

slow down, humanity, slow down!
you run roughshod over soft ground;
over stream and mountain, bird and bee;
over many things you cannot see;
over anyone you can't explain;
for the foul, fleeting taste of tawdry gain;

ah...
for what are you toiling, if not to live?
for what are you living, if not to love?
for, what are you loving, if not mankind?
for, are we not wonder and sighs?

slow down, humanity, slow down!
for, no greater calling than this can be found.

i miss you most

i miss you most
when the drowsy
warmth of morning
cools in the breeze
of a busy day;

when tenderness
reaches through toil
to touch me
on the shoulder,
and remind me
that you're there;

when each successive
moment pauses -
then turns to ask me
what you might think
of this, or that,
or everything that is,
or was, or (wishing) ever be;

when the vulnerable twilight
slips past reluctant slumber
into the darkest fits
of wretched night;
then, do i miss you -
your every aspect
and sweetest grace -
oh, so very, most of all.

POETRY

i still wear your scarf

i still wear your scarf around my neck,
over my shoulders and across my chest,
like an ever-present embrace, your arms
of woven and colorful, your feminine looks
good on me;

i find myself absentmindedly caressing
memories from the fabric of our
time together; touching our moments;
lifting you to my face to drown in
all that remains of your scent;

i still wear your scarf around my neck,
nearest my heart,
where it seems happy to be;
and, often, i wonder with a smile,
did you leave it behind
intentionally?

every

every
one
knows,
two too
much
equals
three
(
1hough,
2o
m3,
it's
0nly
3v3r
happ
en'd
thric3
be4
)

i touch taut, trembling tones

i touch taut, trembling tones of silver and gold
suspended above the resonant silence;
what will my fingers conceive?

caressing life from lifeless;
warmth from deathless;
and you from such as me;

i pause to feel the flame;
cold poised upon the point
of touch and feel;

string and movement;
music and sound;

this guitar has known my heart,
and spoken all its secrets most profound.

church bells ring in the distance

church bells ring in the distance,
sacred and sky
swirling sound
over a world
of slumbering gods;

i open my eyes,
through my window
comes, kissing my heart awake,
the aching gratitude of the world's
first love, and the deepest prayer
forms on my lips:

you.

will i ever run out of words

will i ever run out of words
in my striving to explain
the miracle that is you?

only once i've succeeded.

and then,
i will know for certain
that i have failed;

and gladly will i
begin anew.

as we speak, sleep steals

as we speak, sleep steals,
silent and unseen,
into the soft folds
of your darkened room;

like a thief come
to take you from me,
laying hold of precious and rare,
that which i cherish most,
my pearl of greatest worth;

and you fade...
and you wane...

like the graceful moon,
you drift beyond the fingers
of my words, beyond the reach
of my heart, beyond all waking
and i lose you - slipping silence -
dimming lights beneath
the surface of the night,
until morning sets all loneliness aright.

take my words

take my words;
take all that i have written,
all that i have spoken to you;

gather them all together,
and press them to your lips;

let their incense fill your mind,
their weight imprint your soul,
their meaning overflow
the wide contours of your heart;

then, in the chance meeting of our lips,
let all else be utterly forgotten;

for i have yet to speak
with greater eloquence
than our least eloquent kiss.

where do you go?

where do you go?
where do your thoughts take you?
when intently you watch my lips
as i speak with you?

as i lose my point
among the softness
of your eyes?

as i tumble from heights
of discourse and lofty notions
down deep endless caverns of falling,
losing, surrendering myself to you;

if only to spend an hour in your mind...

might it be like glancing a map
of inner landscape and knowing?

how i would emerge as the one man
to have glimpsed the streets of Heaven;

and having seen where i have been,
how could i ever love any
but you alone
again?

oceans bleed moonbeams

oceans bleed moonbeams
drifting out to see
where the edge of the sky will appear:
in the cracks of infernal doom,
at the breaking of the day,
where horizon mends even the most
hackneyed of my pitiful perspectives;

as i so dream, the setting sun sizzles
and sputters great serpents of saline surf,
breathing deep from deep, and lung
by sodden lung;
until only the white, bloated,
flesh of morning remains;

oh, how it chills the marrow
of my will to live,
forming death as a sculptor
forms lifeless in his hands;

in a miracle of awareness,
i lift my fingers to my brow
where hot, wet life clots
against the precious wound
of my greatest unknowing;

would that i had hair to mat
and staunch the flow of dying;
would that i could claim success
from a life of fruitless trying.

POETRY

i dreamed you were perfect

i dreamed you were perfect,
and, oh, how this dream came true; but,
i did not wish you perfect with the vile
imperfections of the world;
nor perfect with the glut of luxuriant,
or the inner vacant of vanity;
if i be honest, not even did i wish you
perfect in the wiles of wanton
(though, this is a dream to be explored);
i seek not such meaningless trinkets;

no, i dreamed you were perfect,
and it could only have been you;
for, perfection is not something
which exists of its own,
it only ever is
when it is
as it was meant to be:
the soul to its mate;

for, apart from that which it completes,
it holds its perfection in readiness;
as a key is perfect only for the door it opens,
or a rhyme waits for its truest couplet,
or a sum knows perfection only at its full worth,
you have been perfect for me, my love,
from the day of my imperfect birth.

you move in me

you move in me,
like thin tufts of
violet smoke,
ghost feathers of
wispy and trembling,
the vapor of your goodbye
coats my every mood;

i'm acrid with the bitterness
of real, the no of wanting,
the lie of apprehension;

whence this vile fume?
whence this sickly regret?

alas! smoke does follow
the pains of fire,
lest this foolish heart
of mine forget.

a gaggle of lost souls

a gaggle of lost souls
in a graveyard
of hollow and hopeless;

bandits behind each glittering,
turning stone -
one armed and snickering -
forging nothing from little
and less from despair;

i watch from too near,
while the world outside
crumbles into a chasm
of yesterday's making;

but i remember far more
than could ever be won
by the throw of the dice
or the pawning of a soul;

though the sniveling world
rotates astride twin poles
of greed and fear,
i recall when giants
lived here.

there is no silence

there is no silence
like that of a winter's morn;

crisp on the bitter wind's
haggard, care-worn face;

probing fingers search
my sinews, driving warmth
and life from each depression;

tempting me simply, effortlessly,
to lie down and let her have her way,

as blanch blue runs white
beneath a deathly moon;

for, there is no silence
like the absence of you.

let the nighttime enfold us

let the nighttime enfold us
like a quilt, stitched square by square,
by ancient hands of knuckles gnarled
and gaunt; let me pull the bleak
darkness around our shoulders,
rest your head upon my chest;

nothing else is that was;
nothing else was but this;
nothing speaks nighttime
as softly as these lips,
for all you are;
nothing,
no nothing at all;

beneath the blanket
of this night, this punctured
canvas of timeless and purple,
of ice pearls frozen among
unkindled fire in an inky sea,
you breathe;

you breathe, and the night sky
leans in close; for it has never
heard anything in all its long
listening, never seen anything
in all its perception, never loved
anyone in all its vast heartbreak
as sublime and beautiful as you.

flesh stiffens, hardens

flesh stiffens, hardens
in the thin, cracked
shell of morning;

the air itself falls
shattered on the ground
at my feet, the hopes
of a winter's day;

all is blue, and that
which could not bear it,
contracts in wrinkles of white woe;

death never looked so tragic,
so harsh, so unforgiving as she does
beneath the stagnant suggestion
of sunlight, it enlivens nothing,
not even a hidden something;

for, as surely as winter follows fall,
there is, in me, no warmth i can recall.

i awakened to find you

i awakened to find you
awakening to find me,
unslept and undreamt,
in cold comfortless of
hardened aware and
softening resolve;
until, much by deeper,
i came to know you well;

but, surprising me with thoughtful,
you shared a longing to sit awhile and,

> (with such silent eyes,
> whose wordless gaze
> one might overlook,
> but for love)

to hold and be held
in the shade of deeper still,
wider yet, unbounded more;
joy was the gift you hid
behind the sweet of surprise;

but know this, my love, and know it to be true:
since the night when first i saw your smile,
i've been endless-soul-gazing with you.

take this fleeting

take this fleeting,
too soon passing,
all but already gone,
shard of always,
lost to the passage
of timeless, eternal,
all there is, ever is now;

and drink it...
consume it...

let it become you,
until it defines you,
be at one with it,
live, love and breathe with it,
this life that you lead in it,
this here, again, now;

for, make no mistake, that
life's not for preserving,
like flowers are hung 'til they dry;

life is for living,
each second, each moment;
each you and i surely will die;
be sure, in the here-time,
the drear as the dear time,
you're, here and now, truly alive.

there is pain in discovery

there is pain in discovery,
and discovery is found in pain;

for, what is suffering, but
a moment beyond our control?
an event not of our choosing?
a will more insistent than our own?
a violent crashing
of immovable realities?

all of which bring us
to the crossroads,
to the intersection
of self and other,
of freedom and captivity,
of anguish and despair,
of delusion and who we truly are;

and it is then that we are
forced to recall
that discovering oneself
is the greatest suffering of all.

oh, my child

oh, my child,
you have grown,
by moment, by instant,
by day, and by you;

with every new try,
and every new brave,
you stretch heart and mind
into you-shapes of new;

and the miracle, child,
is that, just as you grow,
you stay, always,
the same you
i have known.

the snow slips

the snow slips
into beds of evergreen
and autumn's crisp remnants;

each flake an innocent,
untouched soul of God's
most brilliant imagining;

how pure must be
the creases of His mind?

and from my window,
cast in winter blue
and street light orange,
i watch the landscape
growing young,
(as we both do);

while, down below, the inn
wears Christmas, still;

and, though i should be
fast at writing,
weaving wending words
far more prosaic than these,
i cannot help but fall in love
as God's love, everywhere,
falls sweetly through the trees.

where do i begin?

where do i begin?
where you end.

where the you-ness
of all that is not me
thins and fades
and feathers out
into invisible fingers
of infinite everything;

where pastel horizons run
watercolor obscurity
into black, thirsty seas
of skyless and everywhere;

where snowflakes dance
the insatiable air,
their toes of lace and longing
too sore to touch
the solid ground;

where the real
of undeniable now
floods and overflows
with all that came before;

how empty now and i
and we would be
without you
here with us;

where do i end?
where you -
in all your
tiniest ways -
so wonderfully
begin.

POETRY

why does beauty sting the heart, so?

why does beauty sting the heart, so?

i cannot look upon it, but i ache
to embrace its essence within my own;

to be overwhelmed to the point of surging
beyond the tight seams which bind me;

to burst forth and watch as the rills
which once were the river of my soul
seep through the cracks and crumbs
of commonplace, unsightly me;

to be absorbed like wine in a sponge,
or rather, that i myself am the sponge,
thirsty to drink deep of beauty's
intoxicating vintage;
surrendering consciousness
to all that is more than i;

what is it in beauty
that annihilates the mind?

could it be that we stand
too near the flame
giving light
to all mankind?

you are so close

you are so close,
i can almost see you
just over the horizon; barely five miles
between the meeting of our fingertips,
if we stretch, as we always seem to do;

twenty-five thousand twelve-inch strides
in which to count the reasons why
i love you (an oft-used phrase, for sure -
and you *can* be sure, my love,
of this and so much more);

at times, i feel as if i'd crawled
over every stone of hillside and meadow,
bare-kneed and snowy-burdock,
just to sit a while, a ways away,
awaiting always the off-chance
of your smile; like the promise of sunset:

at times, bleak and hopeless;
at times, splitting the pastel sky
in panoramic expanses of elation;
shattering the evening with endless hues,
awash in all the wild wonderful
nuances which describe you;

but who could describe you?
when words are merely breath,
and the sky itself
can only ever hope to hold

the changing moon in its arms
of nothing-blue;

to hold the changeless you...

for i think of all the ways
in which you are you;

all the myriad ways
you find to be you;

simply to be...

for you take pains,
sweet one,
you take pains to be –

without corners cut
or ruses of brevity –

and now your pains
encompass me, too:

                    deliberate -
            mindful -
     intentional –

you endeavor
simply to be...

and be with me...

and still remain wholly you;

...and i miss you,

over the horizon; barely
an arm's-length away;

as the moon is missed
by empty skies

on an all-too-sunny
winter's day.

i must no, more often

i must no, more often;
i must not now;

i must not surrender
my space, my time,
my focus, my will to live
without a fight;

i must not let plunder
these meddling curiosity-
seekers of self in others' pain;

i must not let them pick through
the quivering nerves of raw
and violet, throbbing clumps
of all that has become
so painfully me;

i am more than they see,
far more than they seek;

infinite sums of self
they could never contain,
when they themselves
could barely contain
a drop in the ocean
of depth;

a sliver of
the forests of meaning -

every tree of which
they'd gladly lay low
for the thrill
of the chop;

but could they
then stand tall
in the winds
that would blow,

in generosity of spirit,
i allow, i do not know.

POETRY

why should i wonder, as i do?

why should i wonder as i do?
why would i be surprised?

when lost souls suffer
the anguish of their scars;

the want of their nothing;
the madness of their own
humanity?

why, when i, myself,
wander this world,
agape and blank-faced,
staring straight through
the eyes of calamity;

we are blinded
by the smothering
blanket of self -
self,
always
the self;

its insidious whisperings
soothe us to sleep;

sleep us to ruin;

rend us to death;

consign us to everlasting;

if we could but
tame these tendencies;

slay these dragons;

gut these vile demons;
we might, before
the final trumpet's call,
know love's own
boundless freedoms.

i am a pulsing vein

i am a pulsing vein
through which courses
every drop of you;

the round, tireless
beating of my breast
propels your every
aspect to the site
of my singular wound -
binding and loosing,
like the Keys of the
Fisherman, himself;

that i might seek salvation,
sanguine and serene;
or die upon love's frontier,
within tragic sight
of your shores;

pierce me, and i will bleed
venomous as a summer sunset
snagged like a limp balloon
upon a toothy peak
of snow and colorless;
alone it pines,
for it knows no other way;

stab the specter of my mind,
and i rupture, jagged
as the devil's smile;

sudden as death's
remembrance;
cold as madness feigned;
adieu, adieu, remember me;

staunch this flow of yearning,
(i implore you) and life pools into
puddles at your feet, where
hope and hopeless mingle
like adversarial oil and water;
what colors glaze
the ripples of desire;

no, my love, your hands know
no such violence; they caress
the caverns of my soul; flooding,
washing, making whole that which
time and tide have brutally flayed;

for you are my healing lifeblood,
my continuous heart-song,
my soul's remedy for which
i so earnestly prayed.

lungs flail

lungs flail,
kick panic
in the deep
bottomless saline
of putrid yellow;

i taste the fabled virus;
swallowing hard a lump
of larynx, bruised
by sharp,
angular obstruction;

my flesh, a holocaust
of burnt offerings, runs
wet with flame; red with chill;

i am consumed, a hollow
shell, in which rattle mere
fractures of lucidity, bare
chunks of insanity;

fever's pitch tightens
the skin of feet
and forehead;

i am become a withered
sack of metallic thirst,
a cracked wineskin of
parched and dry mouth;

in my chest, an ocean
swells to expel the gasps
of drowning shallows;

these ribs constrict
like fists of witless rage,
shattering the oaken thwarts
and collapsing the keel
of my quivering hull;

i go down, seek me no more
among the feckless living;
but, with our final breaths,
exchange with me
forgiveness, forgiving.

POETRY

if i could but rest my lips

if i could but rest my lips
against the snowy meadow
of your graceful forehead,
where winter wears white's
pure passion with more elegance
than a bride in her maiden blush,
and darkness o'erhangs the hillside
like the forest eaves, i would know
joy again; i would find peace;

if i could but feel the thoughts
of your heart, see them dance
across your subtle, most subtle
smile, then come to rest
like doves (wild, untamed,
unspoiled by inhibition)
in the branches of my mind,
i would find hope again;
i would learn wisdom;

then, closing my eyes,
i'd see the voice
of your heart,
and decide, at once,
to endure no more
life lived apart.

i am my father's son

i am my father's son,
my mother's child,
but i am not them;

their lives were noble
beyond compare,
but they were not
mine to live;

their challenges,
their struggles,
all fashioned for
and fastened to them
like sculpted fingerprints
of unrepeatable identity;

but mine are mine alone;
and theirs are theirs, and gone;

their joys, their sorrows,
their love, all played out
according to time and temper,
belief and convention,
and the innermost secrets
of their hearts;

how could i know?
how could i but guess?
and what could they know of mine?

my sins and failings;
my faults and falsehoods;
regrets, battles, and surrenders;

theirs, too, are hidden from sight;
theirs, like mine, they longed to put aright;

what did i know of these two simple souls?
what, but the love they gave?
what else matters, in the end?
what, indeed.

for, they were but human,
for all their stature; human,
and nothing more;
but, oh their noble fire,
not a single drop less!
an epitaph to be desired.

and i wonder,
as i sit and ponder, here,
would they say they knew
the son they reared?

at the end of my life

at the end of my life
spent chasing a dream,
a paycheck, a pension,
prestige, or a plan;
and building a family,
now grown - gone before;

having long labored in vain
to stock the shelves
of my mind with facts,
and figures, and words,
and wants upon useless wants;

i come, at last, to the end of my days;

and, selling it all, give the money
to the poor, that they, too,
might learn its utter futility,
as i embark upon life anew:

i want a small, simple home
overflowing with love,
and cats, and laughter, and love,
and music, and you, and (i'll say it)
more cats, and these poems,
and love ever-old, ever-new;

and room for far less of me, my love,
and far, far more of you;

i want mornings that dawn to the sound
of your breathing; and evenings
spent holding your hand; and nighttime,
spent praying thanksgivings to Heaven,
for the gift i could never deserve;

i want moments spent searching
the meadow for flowers, with cameras
and journals in hand; and to sink to my knees
in the warm, northern breeze,
when vast miracles, we observe;

i want days, while they linger;
and weeks, while they're ours;
and months we might gather as years;

for, with you,
all that's dark
is but half-shades, my love;

all that's bright
is most brilliantly clear.

Susan, you may never know

Susan, you may never know
all that your words have said to me;
the imprint each one made
in the soft clay of my supple mind;
shaping, forming, drying, with time;
nourishing me like sunlight
in a newborn leaf;

as a child, i was moved
by the beauty of your life:
a daughter, a teacher, by day;
a bohemian poet, by night;

or so i thought i saw,
from the classroom of my mind,
where scribbling and striving,
i sought to make you proud,
while you encouraged
and gently guided me along;

at your feet, i learned from
j.j. and hayden and
was caressed by "such small hands,"
like rain, softening the fertile
furrows of the sapling writer
inside; but you coaxed him out;
put a pencil in my hand;
and made me believe
i had something to say;

i was struck to the heart
by *Pouring Small Fire*;
the poignant imprint of a tailbone
left behind in the cushion
of your father's chair;
my God, but these words
never left my side!

and now, the way each day
becomes of poem of paint,
of colors, of lines, of wordless grace;
you evolve, as the timeless artists do;
you evolve, becoming ever more you;

looking back, now i see,
that you taught me, above all,
by the grandeur of your selfless heart,
to fashion my life -
as you fashion your own -
as an ever-changing work of art;

and i recall, you once wrote that
my words would reach thousands;
and, somehow, you knew;
yes, somehow, you knew;

but i would not have thought it
a failure, dear friend,
if my words had only reached
your kind heart, in the end.

Dedicated with gratitude to Susan Manchester, teacher, mentor, and friend.

skin blisters and cracks

skin blisters and cracks,
peeling away from pale flesh still
clinging to ribs of bleached and bruised;

flaking in sinewy strips of wet decay;
the southern sun mars all that is fair;

belly up, it languishes on the sand;
i've half a mind to throw it back,
let the waves have their way;

let salt and surf gnaw
its ragged bones bare;

like dry rot in wormwood,
it yields to the relentless winds;

sifting silt and sawdust
between thumb and forefinger;

slowly surrendering itself beneath the callous
indifference of a sallow-faced sky;

oarless, it founders, with no purpose
but to kindle a fire for roasting clams;

its long memory dashed to pieces on the shore;
abandoned by its owner, evermore, evermore;

and i wonder at its name, *The Weather Eye*;

would it feel its final state fair payment
for a life of labor upon the splintering seas?

for every hook and blade that scarred
its wooden hide? did it sense its doom
approaching on the untimely tide?

or, blindsided by faithless apathy,
did it see, in the end, its noble name belied?

infinite in reach, beyond knowing

infinite in reach, beyond knowing
and lifespan; a subtle avalanche
of one sees rounded peaks level
to valleys wide; momentum
makes waves in their wake;

nearer than conscience, they began;
pebbles dropped through glassy skin
disturb the status quo, unseat
the stale stagnant; still waters
breed only decay;

what multiplies quite so much,
so many, so magnificent a factor
as virtue? what multiplier, but love,
could hope to yield
such products as these?

where obstacles arise, they part,
then passing, reengage, unmoved;
not even the encircling shore
can long withstand its rhythmic surge;
but, ceding something of itself,
returns all waves from whence they came;

and, what of the pebble?
and, what of the hand?
content, they sink into slow
obscurity; buried beneath the crushing
weight of ages; time presses onward,

downward, and in on all things,
forming diamonds from common
and memories from men -
from whose small stones of kindness
eternal ripples begin.

green gloss of wax unfolds

green gloss of wax unfolds
from (clenched) within fur-capped
mollusks; the sunlight touches all
things - like a child in a candy shop -
raining wrappers of consumed
and discarded through a pale,
powdery sky; how bashful beauty
is, when coaxed from safe haven;
how searing the light of exposed;

fists relent, letting fall
the grains of hopeful harvest;
enraptured servants ferry far
to find a mate for every bloom;

(but do they travel half as far
as i for love of you?)

these blossoms brook
not an early spring;
for feeble are the shoots
of seeds too hastily sewn;

listening, i hear the trees
lengthening, toes to twigs,
and trunk to tawny limbs;
they stretch the timbers
of their winter stiffness,
feel sap run thick as glue
within paper veins; their trembling

fingertips tickle tiny wings at work
sanding the corners of the wind;

i train my lens upon a blade;
a solitary sentry stands,
rash as a straight razor
in a nursery of innocence;

upon its point, a crimson bead,
a pinprick of speckled black
and bloodied, a prehistoric
pygmy poses for the shutter's eye;

i hold my breath to steady my hand,
and draw my focus on his wing;
while, in the trees, a single leaf
unfurls the first flag of spring.

i shall not, beloved, else but strive

i shall not, beloved, else but strive
(everywhere, in every way)
to sing this heart full voiced and pitiful -

from the peaks of joy wandering
through the valleys of passion below

in and among the thickets
life's tragedies have planted

(i would not dream to lift a blade or clear a path
more beaten than those made by the saline rains,
rivulets of self-awakening)

and over the gardens we tend, we two,
of wildflower and remembrance, i will sing -

that, echoing through our days,
it might grow to such a symphony
as the world has never known.

POETRY

the trees stagger

the trees stagger, stepping from their shower,
with long hair bedraggled and unkempt;
a snarl of snakes matted to shoulders of timber;
even their trunks run wet with spring;

under nails, caked brown and grimy, they
squish March between tuberous toes;
while the frost churns mudshakes of thick
and earthy - worm sprinkles and butterfly
crunch; winter cravings are ravenous;

all around them, cattails call; whistling
wanton to the modest elm, still clinging
to her leaves like a new-fallen Eve;
the wind pranks even the purest;
show me innocence inviolable,
and i will call it a dream;

swollen like a crepe-paper pom-pom,
the soggy hawk drips haughty
in the face of God; his red tail,
a solitary bruise on a body
of beige, puffed and motionless;
each solitary eye sweeps the bent
landscape, his brain making sense of it all;
what prey (tell) would brave this rain
just to die at the end of a beak?

swift clouds, like lead balloons
of billowing flab, entangle themselves

among the branches; sagging like old age
around the ankles of alder and ash;
a moment, they glisten like sugar on the lips,
before the chill, evening breeze
squanders shapeless to mist.

i picked a path through fallen leaves

i picked a path through fallen trees;
corpses strewn across a battlefield
running thick and sloppy with untyped mud;

i stepped gingerly, careful to observe
inordinate reverence; i've always harbored
safe superstitions; one never knows.

all around: the gore of a generation
spilt and splattered in the unkempt grass;

a stern forest's tender youth,
their final springtime
come and gone too soon -
always too soon –

and, powerless to halt the conquering foe,
decay did win the sodden field - triumphant
for a time - to bloat upon fleshless bones.

appalled, the scene affects me more deeply
than the death of a brother; perhaps
it is the violence of their passing;
or the innocence of their lives;

no matter; impoverished as i am,
i fall to my knees, among their stripped
and ravaged remains,
to search the ancient senseless
and maybe find a reason why;

there, pinned beneath the stump
of old Alder's skull,
his teeth of jagged leaves agape,
i found a sapling crushed and maimed,
its stem hobbled by the weight of its elders;

and, removing its burden,
i held aloft what still remained
of this small, frail, fragile hope;

and wept, among hostile strangers,
to hear its needless goodbye.

POETRY

spring... it visited me

spring... it visited me, just moments ago!
a season too soon; six weeks away,
from the groundhog's shadow;

how it startled the winter starling
to see a sparrow at the window;

what would the lank wild turkeys say?

and what a difference these
unexpected degrees do make;

a world at odds with the melting snow;
it drips and runs into pools
of December and January; sorting
itself by month and meaning:

these drops from Christmas past;
these here, remember New Year's best;
but i think it goes ill with poor February,
always at a loss for days;

the mud meanders, restless in its sleep,
only to freeze again upon winter's return;

in waves and ripples of flourishing,
it won't be caught off guard
when the music of nature's chaos
stops; see how the deer leave footprints
by the feeders - the squirrels litter

liberally, for their gentle friends' sake;

this moment of sudden spring cannot
last beyond the nodding of a winter's
dream; even summer is but a cleft
in the frozen year; a calm in the snowfall;
a season come too late, and gone too soon;

for, what is winter, but a drowsy dimming
of the sun's last rays? the world asleep,
enwrapped in sheets of soft, flannel grey.

For my good friend, Patricia Arre. Thank you for lending me the opening line and the imagery of the beautiful creatures who visit your backyard.

you whisper movement

you whisper movement
in the depths of meaning;
revealing a cosmos hidden
in among the seeds
of a soft and single
springtime dandelion;

with tiny eyes,
you see much more
than worlds contain;

beneath the storm clouds
of slate and ominous, you drink
deep the living rain; like Dionysus,
pouring joy into the cellars of my heart;

or as Erato -
with golden arrows in your wake -
you fan and kindle inspiration
for this my tortured art;

when every word begins,
and ends, and rhymes with you,
may i truly claim them as my own,
or would it be untrue?

ah, but you dance divine
with the feet of fair Terpsichore!
painting line and color,
in fleeting flashes, on the wind;

yours, the morning breeze, my love;
yours, the chorus of the evening;
yours, the voice i hear
when all is hushed;

my muse;
my heart's own messenger;
my well of profound and inexhaustible;

bless me, now and always,
and i shall dedicate
my all to you.

let us weave springtime in winter

let us weave springtime in winter,
with threads of laughter and feathers
of robin's breast, red-hued fragrance;

the scent of new rain and old, drowsy
earth; we look good together, my love,
we two; weaving springtime, while
knitting strands of me and you;

let us walk barefoot through the greens
of tall-bladed youth; through the blues
of sky falling in curtains
of cloud and boundless;

the scent of your skin,
caressed and rising
in waves of passionate sunshine;
i taste the salt of your everywhere kiss,
and recall no more than noon;

let us hold romance by the hand,
your pinky cupped and cradled in my lips -
if i could but find a smaller you, i'd hide her
here, too, and never think to wonder why;

only then could we say goodbye;
(until - too late - held secret
in the pockets of our hearts,
we let our old selves
slip through the tears);

even so...

let us weave ribbons from morning
and bind evening to longing, until
springtime has righted all that winter
got wrong; and, barefoot, we lie
in the shade of clouds forming
humming such (simple)
subtle heart songs.

the withered, black pearls

the withered, black pearls
cling to the branch;
dried warts upon
a witch's nose; shriveled
in upon themselves
like the damned,
they have no love left;

even the birds,
in the throes
of winter's want,
pass them by
without a second glance;

they see in them no kindness
to satiate their needs;
they will not break their beaks upon
such useless stones as these;

rank with spite,
they are an obscenity;
a monstrosity
of nature's thwarted purpose;

giving nothing of themselves,
their short lives
dwindle to ruinous
hoarding; all will be
lost by spring;

in the harsh
thirst of desiccation,
i reflect upon my own life,
now nearly spent,
too many fruits of which
hang dead upon the tree;

and i find, in time,
among the fallen leaves,
how stiff and rigid i've become,
a leathered soul beneath
a cruel and thankless sun.

she crouches in shadow

she crouches in shadow; eyes flare,
smoldering like green flames in a shroud
of smoke and acrid; trapped,
scheming; her danger increases
with desperation; poised of subtle
movement, she flicks signals
off the tip of her cunning tail;

i fear for my life, in the long
watches of the night.

beneath the tree, he forages,
unaware; my conscience pricks
to warn him; but something primal
stays my hand; something shameful;
as if i were a calloused, betting man,
and life was but a die to be thrown –

i give him one chance in six;
i've wagered here before.

i wonder, does he even see her?
is it excess of confidence or
fool-heartiness? or are his
nerves as still as breath
on a windowpane?

i press my nose against
the balance of fate playing out
before me, wondering whom

Darwin might prove the fittest.

stilted and restive, he flits
and jitters among the fallen seed;
each eye seeing but a single side
of the story in which he plays
the tragic starling role.

a pounce, a flutter, escape
through the sky; crushed,
this backyard panther
sees her murderous
plot take flight.

snow falls up so downy

snow falls up so downy,
drift, floating; slow motion
flurry of pillow fight clouds;

cottony cough
of sweet baby's
breath breezes;

this is how
moonbeams in love
sigh;

windy, swift, swirling
of hurricane whispers
tussles a field of lace
veils through the sky;

angel wing feathers,
translucent in brilliance;

this is where
heavenly things
hide.

i see ghosts, phantoms

i see ghosts, phantoms,
vague shadows of faces in the snow;
i trace the paths of their lives,
among the ruins
where once i played;
as i aged,
all else has decayed;

i hear voices, accents, lilting names;
once familiar as kin,
but now, no more relevant
than i to them;
and what i look for
could not remain;
in a world of shifting differences,
only memories stay the same;

i walk among the headstones,
my God, i knew them all;
she taught me as a little child;
he laughed and called me boy;
i still feel the day she died,
it was then i learned why mourning
doves cry; i had always thought her
above such frailties as death;
we could not have been more wrong -

i must escape this solemn place
where life is drained away,
the dead live on

in sadness entombed,
and the living await their day;
it breeds and feeds upon
nothing but barren despair;

i feel the passage of time,
no place but here,
where time has swept
all things aside;
i thought roots stretched
deep to grasp the ties that bind;
but the forest was cleared
to make room for new things,
leaving only hopeless
and haggard hearts behind;

i know the contrast
that exists; i've traveled
wide beyond my life:
from cold, white heights;
to sea salt channels;
to the cotton coasts
of old time not forgotten;
i've felt the hopeful
sunshine through the rain,
and returned anew,
that i might sow
good seeds again.

POETRY

people make places

people make places,
love creates a home;

laughter makes smiles
that cannot be made alone;

listening makes connections
which create one mind from two;

understanding makes a joy
out of knowing me and you.

this is but a sunset

this is but a sunset;
this is but a night
where withers the waning moon;

this is all the moment, now,
in which i might exist;
there is no more, no greater (here),
and nothing less than this;
no then, and no tomorrow -
which is just delayed today,

a self-delusion

where withers the waning now;

and, this side of forever,
where time metes out the days,
where moments pass
the moment (passed)
we recognize their face;
where moments (passed)
look back upon a lifetime (passed)
away; in time, too late,

we reach a sad conclusion:

where withered the waning day?

POETRY

who are these faces?

who are these faces?
what are these lives?
do they but wander
through their days
of four walls and lidless?
do their souls dare
to climb their enclosures
and spy a world
of new youth and vast limitless?
or has the dire lullaby,
the dread lie whispering,
'nothing more,
nothing more,
take you this,
and nothing more,'
sung their souls to sleep?
there is no soft security;
there is no fair exchange: no
this for a soul, or that for its pain;
there is no (ever) hope of saving a life;
it simply cannot be preserved,
only lived, and lived aright;
as for me...
i'd rather risk it all in being wrong
than succumb to a safe and subtle lie;
i'd rather kill myself in living
than simply live until i've died.

i feel each mile

i feel each mile, each hairs-breadth,
each infinite half-life of space
as it opens up between us;

gaping wounds of want;
love's traumas born bravely;

scars which smooth into newborn flesh
when caressed by your healing hands;

i bleed for you -
a nobler cause there could never be;

i feel each minute, each instant
of separation, each yawning immensity
of now, as it looks back over its shoulder
and sneers at me; loathsome thief;

wretched robber of that which is most
irreplaceably ours; i would arrest him,
if only i could, and throttle now, cruelly,
until it relinquished every moment
we could not together keep;

i feel each striving of my heart,
each yearning, each reaching out
to touch the steady beating of your own;

i feel the vacant hollow your absence
leaves; the cold shadows where once

your warmth burned bright; the bounding
echoes of your voice against the walls
of my all and everything ;

how could it be my choice
to step away from your side?
even if only for a short time?
how could this be?

i feel each hope, each promise
we exchange, each and every sacred vow
awaiting patiently; each spoken syllable;
the meaning they contain;

how we hand our hearts,
and souls eternal, trembling
vulnerably: mine i give to you;
yours you give to me;

no safer place exists, my love,
we know with certainty;

i feel each breath, each inhalation,
each slow deflation, every settling
of myself into my thoughts;

no tumult; no storm clouds;
no wild emotions obscuring sight;

only memories of you to hold,
until i can hold you tight.

you said it best, my love

you said it best, my love;
with fewer brushstrokes
than my own unsteady hand
could paint this muddled mind;

you sketched in sweet perfection
how our kisses have become
'a slow voyage into a beautiful space,
a space that goes on forever;'

oh but, is this not the space
we hollow out within each other's heart?
endless as deathless eternity;
unbounded as the spheric sky;
untrammeled by wings
of windless ethereal;

we brush aside the veil of awe,
a moment; barely touching;
as, all around us, heavenly
things hold sway;

and, in this space
of endless discovery,
where forever finds
its start, we voyage
through the many
lovely seasons
of the heart.

POETRY

'we're higher than the clouds,'

'we're higher than the clouds,'
the little girl squealed,
without a thought for how,
or a fear of mortality;

nose pressed, lips smudging
the foggy plexiglass;
nothing between her
and 36,000 feet of open wonder;

mother adjusted her earbuds,
rolled her eyes and sighed –

whoever waxed poetic
about a mother's love
found no inspiration here -

'why is everything so little?'
the child asked, chin hooked
over the headrest, eyes
wide with innocence,
she'd moved on
from mother to me;

'you got bigger!' i replied
(in truth, i lied)
but for a moment
she believed me,
looking hard at herself

(something mother
could never do -
nor i, at me, it's true);

'nooooo!' she exclaimed,
then forgot me and turned
back to her window seat-
view from 3C, where I knew
she thought me very silly;

and from behind, i could hear
a frail voice of many years,
say, 'i never did like to fly;'

it was the very same child,
some seventy years hence;
and i wondered what had changed,
between fear and innocence;

what the child had lost,
or what the old woman
had achieved;
and if wonder, once lost,
might ever be retrieved.

the cardinal puffs his plumage like a pout

the cardinal puffs his plumage like a pout;
it's been a long winter
among the muddy meadows;

since spring has just arrived,
the southern sun now
sucks the puddles dry;

but he's just in time;
the sluggish rainwater runs
brown from his breast;

i half expect his scruffy feathers
to bleed red;
the white, winter sky
has bleached him so;

the earthworms emerge
braver than i recall;
or is it that the rain has floated
all their fears away, their cautious concerns,
their homes and all their worm-worn trinkets?

with nothing left to lose,
they risk it all, and count it very little,
beneath a perilous sky;
i've known such disregard before;

who will clean up
all this stale and useless?

last year's clothing cast down
and tossed aside; is it not wasteful
to wear but once?

there's barely room allowed
for the newborn leaves -
who arrange, with helpless hands,
the dry bones of the old;
their bodies not yet cold;
nor this my soul;
nor this my soul.

you always start my day

you always start my day
with joy, my love;

as sure as the sunrise kisses
the morning sky, you kiss
my mind awake; and, stretching
its arms to fingertips tingling,
my heart smiles to be loved;

do the morning birds always sing
so sweetly as this?

you always begin in me with joy, my love;
in the scent of dark aromas, i stir;

i need no more stimulant
than your gentle voice, sweet one,
cascading as it does
through my every breath;
i feel you, always, in me,
with me, and ever beyond me;

can morning dawn without a sunrise?
can daytime bloom beneath the moon?
could there, in my heart, be ever joy
apart from you?

we always end our days with love,
dear heart;

in the lengthening shadows
of an aging day, you settle into
my every awareness, like nothing
i have ever known;

for you have become
my morning,
my evening,
my every joy,
and truest home.

winter bloom

winter bloom, you surprise me;
peeking out from among the leaves
where autumn sought to conceal you;
where springtime sought to preempt you,
in all of her fragrant finery;
but you answered them both
with silent snowfall, clothing
the world in ever new; and ever you
rouse me from dismal sleep;
for, in the evening of my life,
i had pulled the days and months
around my shoulders like a quilt
of drafty and moth-worn, but familiar,
oh yes, thin-comfortingly familiar;
but where is comfort to be found,
if not where hearts, in love, are bound?

winter bloom, the snow will not hurt you;
it wraps you in a cloud of care;
sheltering all that is delicate and precious
from the jealous glare of unbeautiful;
from the prodding fingers of unkind;
from all that would unspeak you,
or erase you from heart and mind;
for it seems some loves
only take root in the snow,
the better their immortal
fragrance to bestow.

on winter waters

on winter waters, in waning fall,
with no destination, no goal at all,
no where, no when,
no whom, nor how,
no promise to keep
no sacred vow;

i seek only the wind,
carried on by the waves,
beneath sun and sky,
the faint whispering ways
of clouds as they pass
so curiously by,
sweet, gentle hearts
looking down from on high;

i would learn all their thoughts
and the cares of their minds,
the secrets they've learned
beyond age out of time,
steep my soul in the whats,
and the wheres of the wise,
and the truths only learned
from their whispering sighs;

but the winter takes hold,
in the waning of fall,
and the day is not mine,
no not mine at all.

wildflowers

why wildflowers, i wondered,
and fathomed the deep places of your heart;
as if i might touch your mind
or hope to taste the fragrance of your soul;

> undaunted hope strives
> toward phantoms of chance;
> (poor, foolish thing)

but to hold you closer,
to embrace your essence
in these finite arms
is all hope might need to find joy -
if even these hopes be dreams;

> why wildflowers, i wondered,
> then, blushing, demurred -
> why, dear heart, it must be,
> i see now at last,
> that your heart is a prairie-wide
> (secrets of endless hills
> rolling on into vistas so green)

that wildflowers should feel
right at home in your soil, where,
pretentious, the rose or the pale
fragile lily would surely wilt
beneath the warmth
of a heart such as yours.

whom does the moon love

whom does the dawn love
more than you?

the sky, aflame with bold and silhouette,
pastel extravagance of tortured displays?

or is it the earth whom he loves,
in taupe and ochre tangible?

or the sea, with wild untamed passion,
where deep roils upon deep,
and all hope is lost to the darkness?

whom does jealous dawn love
more than you?

in truth, he answers,
no other could it be:

for the lover
seeks a beloved
greater than he.

let's take the next plane

let's take the next plane to
Anywhere, Neverbeen, or Paris -
(it being autumn and time being
not yet come to pass);

i've Neverbeen, Anywhere,
but Paris
is right where I left it

last,
       last,
              there must Neverbe
      a last!

for Nowhere else will do;
(except exquisite Prague, perhaps);

oh, to see it all with you!

or see it's reflection in your eyes,
without the distraction of Anywhere;

it being tomorrow
and time being determined
to leave us all behind.

show me (my darling)

show me (my darling),
show me the countries
you have called your home;

show me all the soft,
small corners (my darling)
upon which you have laid your head:

beauty-painful; joyful-agony;
never mine (death-hopeful) –

but show me without pictures,
without words, without me at all

(oh how i do tend to
get in the way of things meaningful)

show me only with your eyes, your own;
your thoughts, so wise; your feelings,
broken, mended, healing;

(oh how life does tend to
get in the way of living)

(my darling), take me with you
that i might not be left behind;
and so, at last, be free to find
all countries hid inside your picturesque mind.

POETRY

know me gradually

know me gradually;
unhurried, we must be;

create this
(bit by little, and little by more)
could it be? love?

*(to whisper is to scream it;
once said, we can't unsay it)*

new life, new change, becoming Us;

so, better just to know me, gently;

don't let me be
hastily, impatiently - adverbedly –

(for life is short, forsuredly)

but while i wrote these words for thee,

so gradually, unknownst to me,

we tripped and fell *(undoubtedly)*

in love.

please do not shield me

please, do not shield me,
please, do not protect me;

i fear an iron cage (lifeless)
far more than supple death;

the melting (sudden!) loss of self
amidst a sea of safe and nameless;

the acceptance of wary distance
in place of warm connection;

a drowsy, listless numbness
in place of wild abandon;

for,
the highest good
is not life
lived
at all cost;
but life
well-lived
and joyful.

i have known nothing, too long

i have known nothing too long;
nothing of you, nothing much of me,

nothing of the way
you brush back your hair
while telling me of Switzerland;

i have known nothing too long,
to be suddenly, haphazardly
face to face with
such graceful remembrance;

oh, how my own life should be
mercifully forgotten,
to make room for something new,

for i have known only me, too long,
and should have rather known only you.

love? do you think

love?
do you think your hand
was made for mine?

it fits so well,

(finger-laces tied up
in neat, little bows);

whence this warmth,
this comfort-completeness,

this "of course, it had to be you"?

have i held your hand forever, love?

or is this really new?

look closely

look closely,

> see how skillfully
> i talk myself down
> from the ledge?

balancing,
reasoning,
dredging emotion

> into sandbags,
> until a path opens
> through the waves & foam

(see how i mix my metaphors)

and, relieved again,
i follow it
back to
you.

how can i sleep?

how can i sleep?
how can i soothe these thoughts?
for i, too, sit silent-alone in the dark, sometimes;

    (shhh... fool that i am; hush, beloved fool)

        "there is no monster 'neath your bed
        more menacing than he inside your head;
        what? does this thought fail to soothe?"

"yea, forsooth, save only sleep;
naught else could fish me from the deep.

"from the deep, from the deep,
by God, pray, save me from the deep;
from overthinking, under-sleep;
for now i lay me down to weep."

        but, even prayer falls far afield,
        when hearts are used as living shields.

may we always love

may we always love
with hearts that perceive:

your quick, stolen smile,
(concealed by your hand)
as you sip the wine of our conversation;

the tilt of my head as i lean into the deep
pools flowing from your heart;

the stories of those around us;

the feelings of those we love;

the God Whose hand it was
cast the sun and moon, the stars and sky,
the earth and you (and even me)
into elegant and irrepressible motion;

may we always love
with hearts that perceive
that love grows when given,
all the more to receive.

are you not the rain?

are you not the rain?
(i know you of old; more recent, of late)

are you not she who waters all things,
making greening things grow?

are you not tiny, like droplets that
...tickling... find furious paths to the sea?
are you not she?

i've seen your arrival,
watched,
waited,
observed;

i've longed to be drenched,
but in patience, i've learned that
no man could hope summon
that which, precious, is earned;

if you are the rain,
then, in time,
you'll return.

you move through me

you move through me with
unsought breezes of introspection,
stirring crumbling leaves
into eddies of change;

('consider this' being the brave door
opening onto 'who knew?')

and who, indeed?

but the more you move through me,
the more (i fearful) become myself,
and i do so want to be me,

or any man you love
quite so much.

let's plan to make no plans tomorrow

let's plan to make no plans tomorrow,
instead, we'll let the snow decide,

flake by flake, and blizzard by blizzard,
until, buried deep in soft, fluffy, forgetful,
the day passes into silent night;

and then, beneath cool darkness,
we'll pull a blanket
of shimmering sky

(descending everywhere,
alighting with bare, blue feet)

over our heads, and snuggle down
into the downy snowfall,

float so falling, silken dreams rise,
while winter remakes the world outside.

wheres

wheres
do not mean
quite as much as
whos
mean just as much
or more than
whys,
they matter
just the same as
hows
will always be
far more than
whats;
i'm certain
that you
would agree.

you tricked me

you tricked me,
that you might love me;

that you might give me
that which i would not receive;

such was the darkness of my heart;
such was the blindness of my mind;
such it was, but you would not endure
the self-injuring of my self-servitude;

instead, you chose to self-endure
such injury and base servitude
as this, for the sake of my self,
fool that i am and ever will be;

you tricked me, that you might love me;
you made my haughtiness of rejection
a cunning prank of love;

for you were ever dying to love me,
one who did ever owe you his love.

POETRY

is love not pure?

is love not pure?

is love not stainless
as a winter sky?

is love not clear as truth
in an angel's mind?

does it not silence self,
and bid all storms subside?

and, oh, what love endures;

does love not...

make the heart
a fragile song?

but, of the mind,
a fortress, strong?

when emotions fade,
the will prolongs

a love
that was
loved as pure.

the nighttime stains my bare feet

the nighttime stains my bare feet
red with smudged iniquities;

the best of me lingers still
among the brutal daylight;

a tardy reminder of
a month of mondays
spent naming raindrops —
once plumes of evanescence —
as they razed their liquid souls
against a skin of moon and skylight;

(warm your feet against me, love,
what good is this fire, if not
to fashion your sanguine smile?)

watch as the day turns,
discreet as a maiden's sigh;

how shrewdly tomorrow comes,
collecting payment
on a lifetime deferred;

only such would presume
to place a price on ruin;

only such as these would
make it their delight;

i cannot; i lack the heart;
i lost it, once, among the trees;

(do you recall
when first i fell?

so lost in love
of your
footprints
in the snow?

But you didn't know;

how could you,
though?

i ever feared,
too much,
to show).

spare me

spare me;
never let me
believe the narrative;

ever let me know the truth;
and knowing, choose living;

there's a mystique to the magic;
a mysterious underline;
a meaning for the taking;
interpretation in every mind;

but the words are mine,
only mine; all mine;

i choose them for reasons
which none (nor i) could show;

but i speak them all to you,
Sandra; this truth, you surely know;

each word, a ship
set sail from my lips
a journey to your heart,
over high seas
of time and in-between;

we chart each cove,
each island oasis,
each tiny paradise

of our own making;

the world made safe by its creator,
for unbridled discovery;

and though the ears of
gulls and dolphins
strain each syllable
fine as sand;

they do not yet understand;

they might never understand,

that you are but the fairest heart,
and i am but a man.

feel the brevity of life

feel the brevity of life,
as i have from my youth;
the tight grip of urgent;
the shallow gasp of fleeting;

are we not in haste?
do we not fail to
outpace the inevitable?
are we not dogged by death?

at the bottom of this hill
of brakeless unstoppable,
a brick wall looms against frail
mortality; a hard stop against hope;
there is no padding,
no safe conduct,
no avoiding
the soul's release;

my hands are too slick
with mortal dismay to grasp
this final doom; but it is there,
always there; i fear it not,
damned bully; oh where is thy
victory? oh where is thy sting?

this is not the end of all things,
only all that i have known;
and this i whom i have known;
a me who was mine,

but given, as i was to you;
i do so regret your loss of me;

this is not morbid dread;
i do not pity my lot; no,
this is a clarion call;

a warning reminder
that time does not age,
but dies as readily
as it is born;

therefore, make no plans,
for there is no tomorrow,
only today in which to live
all love, all joy, all sorrow.

love is too singular for rhyme

love is too singular for rhyme;
harmonizing, still, with all that is true;

love is the solvent universal -
breaking, bonding, watering
the arid expanses of now;

kindling the leveling fires of passion,
creation, stoic resolve - but ever unfailing kind;

with patience, it sweeps away all weeds,
and seeds the soil where beauty grows;

love wears its smile, constant and calm,
ever in the eyes, where smiles curve deepest
and lies cannot hide;

love is the mystery athwart evolution;

love is the nonsense
that makes sense of all things;

love seeks and finds,
she heals and she binds;
love makes the jubilant birds sing.

Mia's wook-wuck

the wook-wuck went wooking
where wardles wonce waddled
in west willow wompus near
whippoorwill way;

when, what to its wonder,
a walker came wandering
and welcomed the wook-wuck
to wook by the bay;

the waves were wash-wriggling,
the whales were all wiggling,
the walruses wallowed
the daylight away;

but, wook-wuck and walker,
who wouldn't wade water,
went back to walk-wandering
all wonesome that day.

For Mia, who hears things in her own way, and lends those things to me. Thank you for inventing the wook-wuck and for introducing us to each other.

please don't

please don't;
do, be still;
be at peace;
hold your life at bay;
restrain this impulse
to run, to bolt, to dash
yourself to fractured
fragments of a tragedy;
your gentle heart,
no more; your noble frame
crushed by man's
inexorable, blunt force
of careless careening;
i decrease, that you might,
in caution, cross; i slow
the closing of our two
paths; i pause to give you
pause; for your mind
is as unpredictable
as a million variables
of need and want,
skill and desire,
instinct and action,
fear and regret;
oh deer one,
please, don't;
not now, not ever;
but, if it must be,
don't live in your youth
death's dread mystery.

this is where my everyness lives

this is where my everyness lives;
beside a stream of sometimes;
vague distant hills of yet to come
cast docile shadows down
piedmont plains;

mistaken, we were
sure of our summit;
but the vaulting spectacle
reveals insatiable valleys between;
and age-worn landscapes
await spring's newest green;

this is where my evermore hides;
astride the back of swift canyons,
forever strives toward unflinching horizons
someone never hoped to find;

see how it snows in the upper reaches
of our bruised and shattered,
laying blankets of innocence
to warm and coddle tender wounds;
no more to fight what love eludes;

this is where my lover sighs;
across fair meadows of wildflower waves
the wind caresses with faintest touch;
the sweet kiss of sunlight
upon your smiling face;

in the snowy evening glow, we swim
through currents of children's laughter -
full-clothed and shivering -
we seize upon this moment,
sign it as our own, wrest from it
all the joy such fragments yield;

for, we are blessed beyond that
which many lives might live,
when the love we've received
grows, the more that we give.

under the cover of darkness

under the cover of darkness,
the storm arrived in the night,
held cruelly by the frozen claws
of lifeless and gripping,
dull-eyed, aching winds;

over and around, above,
and below, whipping through
the wires, hung taut and bouncing,
as they spanned the naked, vulnerable field,
the fiendish wind danced like a troupe
of lost souls, howling, as they streaked
through an eternity of grim despair;

an unending screech of tires
on wet asphalt, a tooth dragged
over the slow, grooved skin of a record,
the wind was wild with wanton hatred;

a demoniac possessed of self-injurious
pleasure; a wart-nosed, wailing hag
being pulled into saltwater taffy, uttering
incantations in the godforsaken void
between despair and springtime;

each feathery snowflake drawn
across the blue, braided strands,
as a rosined bow simpers along
the sinews of a violin string; i awoke;

half-asleep and muttering; cursing
the careless discourtesy of (my God,
is that the wind?!)

i trained my ear in the morning's
most fruitless hours; listening, thrilling;
alive with the passions of living!

greedily coveting each fear;
each annoyance; each stifled breath
of wonder caught captive, and rattling
loose in the cavern of my chest;

i awoke;
let me never
sleep again.

they forage in frozen fields

they forage in frozen fields;
warm, wet noses buried
beneath the prickling snow -
burning, gnawing hot flesh
with crystal blades of ice and
relentless - they suffer
the loneliness of wordless nature,
and bear it all stoically;

at creekside, they bend long,
unburdened backs, to dip
chaste lips in the bruised stream;
trading warmth for life, like toxic love;
this shrewd-cornered, insipid drink
spells the impoverishment of pure

innocence; at play, they make love
from want; joy from pain; life
while hunted; bleeding crimson
against the achromatic snow;
rendering beauty for sport;
there is no sense in wasteful
ruin, only the turmoil of ignorance;

sweet eyes, you notice me
from across the windswept,
wintry plain; in awe,
i shall be silent
and still as the frosty moon;
i seek not to disturb your snowy eve,
grant me only your noble heart to perceive.

you absorb me, like the rain

you absorb me, like rain
through the petals of a rose;
your most delicate touch
lending grace to my vulgar,
as i, little by all, become you;

in the how of my every,
i am rendered more
by the most that you are;
aware of this gradual
unbecoming of all that i was
into all i might become;

lost in the runoff
of your grounding, i etch
a path of passion to the sea;

as if this one droplet could increase
the wetness of an ocean;

the perfections of your truth;

or the sweetness of all that is you
by admixture of all that is me.

this place has suffered enough

this place has suffered enough,
consuming the bodies of those
who made it home; laid to rest,
themselves among the many ruins here;

i lay blame like wreaths at graveside,
passing sentence no one cares to hear;
the dead would disagree;

and why shouldn't they?
for they live here no more,
needing no sustenance
from the fields they'd salted
with blinding greed;

sold at a price of twenty silver coins;
sold at a cost beyond reckoning;
for naught but a lie;

and who can value worthless?
who can redeem innocence?
none but Christ, Himself
exchanged for, few can recall;

and what of those who linger?
what of those who remain
beyond the norm of nature's decay?

they suffer beneath the burdens
of their contemporaries;

injustice bequeathed;
servicing debts incurred
by other's profligacy;
a legacy of dubious deceit;

i seethe with indignation;
recoil with disdain;

behold the beads and baubles,
toys for children;

cheap trinkets for bankrupt souls
slipping slowly beneath the surface
of desperation, lungs gurgling
foam in the void;
what is it you seek to drown?

it all rings clear as a battle cry, to me:

there is no better means
to defeat one's foe
than harnessing his weakness
to deal the final blow.

i've grown old

i've grown old;

as old as
all others my age;

though younger, still,
than those
who came before;

there is thin comfort in youth,
thinner than the waist,
but, less so, the hair;

for, all is relative;

and even they
have grown old,
too.

goodbye, goodbye

goodbye, goodbye
do fare thee well,
goodbye;

for, we shall not
e'er meet again,
do fare thee well,
goodbye;

and when I think
to think of thee,
i'll stop and
wonder why;

for, sadness,
i've no sympathy;

do fare thee well,
goodbye;

my love has made
her home in me,
and there,
she will abide;

so, fare thee well,
for evermore,
do fare thee well,
goodbye.

About the Poet

Matt Pelicano was born and raised in Central New York, the youngest of eight kids.

From his youth, Matt has always loved the poetry of Sylvia Plath, E.E. Cummings, Shel Silverstein, TS Eliot, Walt Whitman, Robert Frost, and William Shakespeare.

His literary heroes include JRR Tolkien, CS Lewis, Oscar Wilde, Agatha Christie, and David McCullough. At age 10, he pulled an old guitar out of the trash, taught himself to play, and soon began writing lyrics, songs, poetry, short stories and books.

A widower, Matt has three grown children, Andy, Joey, and Megan, and splits his time between Upstate South Carolina, Central New York, and traveling. Visit Matt online at: **www.MattPelicano.com**.

www.ingramcontent.com/pod-product-compliance
Lightning Source LLC
Chambersburg PA
CBHW032336300426
44109CB00041B/1074